BICYCLING THE OREGON TRAIL

Don Weinell

Caxton Press

Kate —
After three years, your encouragement and persistence paid off.
You finally convinced me to put my words to paper.
Without you, this book would have never come to life.

Caxton Press

Library of Congress Cataloging-in-Publication Data

Names: Weinell, Don, author.
Title: Bicycling the Oregon Trail / by Don Weinell.
Description: Caldwell, Idaho : Caxton Press, [2017] | Includes
   bibliographical references and index.
Identifiers: LCCN 2017020172 (print) | LCCN 2017023605 (ebook) |
ISBN 9780870046162 | ISBN 9780870046124 (alk. paper)
Subjects: LCSH: Bicycle touring--Oregon National Historic Trail--
Guidebooks.
   | Oregon National Historic Trail--Guidebooks.
Classification: LCC GV1045.5.O74 (ebook) | LCC GV1045.5.O74 W45
2017 (print)
   | DDC 910.9795--dc23
LC record available at https://lccn.loc.gov/2017020172

Cover and book design by Jocelyn Robertson

Printed and bound in the United States of America

CAXTON PRESS
Caldwell, Idaho
197752

BICYCLING THE OREGON TRAIL
Don Weinell

"Public domain image of the Oregon Trail map which appeared in Ezra Meeker's "The Ox Team or the Old Oregon Trail 1852 -1906" Fourth Edition, 1907."

TABLE OF CONTENTS

If you wou'd not to be forgotten,
As soon as you are dead and rotten,
Either write things worth reading,
Or do things worth the writing.

– Benjamin Franklin, 1738

Foreword

In the spring of 2013 I was contacted by email by Don Weinell, a biologist for the State of Louisiana as well as an ornithologist, history buff and long-distance cyclist. Later that spring he planned to complete the second of five, two-week rides retracing the Oregon Trail across the West from the Missouri River at Independence to the Willamette River at Oregon City. This second leg would start in Kearney, Nebraska, and end 600 miles later at Casper, where the trail made the last of its crossings of the North Platte River and where I happen to live.

He arrived in Casper in late June. We had lunch and talked about routes, maps and trail history. The following evening he came to our house for a cookout with family and friends. As he traveled, he posted a daily blog with notes and photos. By the end of the fourth segment, from Pocatello, Idaho, to Baker City, Oregon, he'd begun thinking about turning the blogs into a book. In October 2016 he sent me the fifth and final chapter, and I began reading. What a delight! The friendly, curious man I'd met three years earlier—well, I felt I was having a chance at last to get to know him.

Here in Wyoming we pride ourselves on our empty spaces and wide horizons. We have very few people, most of them in towns scattered along the courses of creeks and rivers. Between the towns we have millions of acres of short-grass prairie and sagebrush steppe, where hardly anyone lives at all. Most visitors hurry across the state to Yellowstone and Grand Teton national parks in our northwest corner. Sometimes, however, people pass through who seem to like the emptiness just for itself. Often they are history buffs, drawn like some of the rest of us to the huge vacancies of our landscapes because they make it so easy to imagine the past. Don, I think, is one of these.

As I read, I grew gradually more and more absorbed by his trip. His sentences are often short, his tone even. As he covers his daily 40 or 50 miles he accumulates details of weather, route and terrain, much as the earlier trail diarists did. We learn about cafés, campgrounds and occasional motels, and even better, we get glimpses of people in the towns, small towns and hamlets the Oregon Trail route passes through today.

Mr. Weinell is so modest he never points it out—but you can tell, too, how carefully he planned. Each night he has a good idea of where he expects to camp. If he has to cross or camp on private land, he always seems to have acquired permission in advance. And people invite him in—to their houses or RVs; even, once or twice, they arrange potlucks around his passage through town.

We also get a quiet history. He manages this largely by means of historical anecdotes about people and events on the historic trails, with the stories strung like beads along his route. So the history is more geographical than chronological; slowly we get a feel for time and distance and the blunt-minded persistence it took him to make the trip—and a feel for similar qualities in the wagon pioneers.

The evening he came to our house it was a Friday at the end of a hectic week. Our two grown sons were in town—the gathering included both their friends and ours. Don, if I remember right, didn't say a lot. Look, I wanted to say to everyone, here is our traveler! But only now, reading his book, do I feel I've begun to know him—his evenness, his ease with solitude, his curiosity about the people and places of the present and the past, his persistence, his sense of humor that is quiet as bicycle tires on brand-new asphalt.

I know you'll enjoy this book.

Tom Rea, president
Wyoming chapter, Oregon-California Trails Association
December 2016

Preface

There was no epiphany. I didn't wake up one morning and decide to ride my bicycle 2,100 miles across half the United States without giving the matter some thought. The decision was a gradual merging of all the possible options that occurred to me over time. My initial plan was to see as many of the historic sites along the Oregon Trail as possible. As I learned more about the trail, I started to realize that it's more than just a collection of isolated points on a map. To understand the trail you have to be willing to connect the dots.

Modern highways follow the route of the Oregon Trail pretty closely. You could easily make the trip from Independence, Missouri, to Oregon City, Oregon, in a week. If you did that though, you'd miss other important aspects of the trail. You wouldn't feel the land and understand why the original travelers chose one route over another. In the air conditioned comfort of your car, you wouldn't fear an approaching thunderstorm. You'd miss out on the constant winds of Wyoming or the summer heat of the Snake River Plateau. In short, you'd see the Oregon Trail, but you wouldn't experience it.

Every year thousands of bicyclists in the United States take off on long rides. Some travel for a day or two, others for months at a time. Since 1976, I've dreamed of doing a cross country trek on my bike. That was the year of our nation's bicentennial. As part of the celebration, an organization called BikeCentennial promoted a cross country ride from Yorktown, Virginia to Astoria, Oregon. I wanted to do it but I was only in high school at the time. It would have to wait.

BikeCentennial eventually morphed into the Adventure Cycling Association. Today it has over 50,000 members, of which I am one. As I thought more about my desire to experience the Oregon Trail firsthand, it just seemed obvious the best way to do it was by bike. Traveling on a bicycle would allow me to see the trail at a slower pace, and I wouldn't have to stay on the pavement. Although a typical road bike has skinny tires that sink deep into soft surfaces, a good touring bike has few limitations. Its wider tires would allow me to follow the original trail even closer.

Time is a consideration. Bicycle travelers tend to fall into one of three categories: students on summer break, teachers on summer break, or retirees. Unfortunately, I'm none of those. I estimated that riding along the entire Oregon Trail would take me about two months if done in one shot. I decided the best way to get started was to divide the trip into shorter bites. Beginning with a few weeks in the spring of 2012 and continuing for a few more weeks each year, I finally made it to the end of the trail in 2016. If I had waited for the perfect time I may never have started.

Since the Oregon Trail is a National Historic Trail, the National Park Service has developed an online interactive map that shows the original trail layered over modern roadways. This map formed the basis of my planning. For even more detail I relied on the expertise of the Oregon-California Trails Association (OCTA). Volunteers of this organization tirelessly research and mark long stretches of the trail. Threats to the trail, and there have always been threats, are monitored by the various state chapters. Members are then mobilized to stand up for trail preservation. I'm also a member of OCTA.

Although bicyclists and amateur historians often travel in different circles, this book proves that our interests can overlap. It's sad that many touring cyclists spend a lot of energy crossing the country without ever really grasping the history of the land they're passing through. Likewise, many history buffs stop just long enough at roadside parks to read the signs then move on as quickly as they arrived. Imagine traveling in such a way that you not only see the countryside but you actually have time to understand it. Such is the magic of a bicycle.

For me, a key to getting the most out of this trek was to make contact with the real experts of the trail. Bill Peterson, the president of OCTA's Nebraska chapter, helped me plan a route that avoided the busiest roads. He also suggested to call certain landowners along the trail for access to historic sites on their property. In Wyoming, OCTA's chapter president is Tom Rea. In addition to reviewing my maps, he gave me a better understanding of the impact of the Mormon migration through the area (Mormons are members of the Church of Jesus Christ of Latter-day Saints, or LDS for short). Jerry Eichhorst serves as OCTA's Idaho chapter president. Prior to starting the Snake River leg of my journey, he shared a lot of advice about the Main Oregon Trail Backcountry Byway. Jerry was instrumental in the creation of this scenic byway and his knowledge of the route is unequaled. As I rode into Oregon, OCTA members Stafford Hazelett and Jim Tompkins gave me valuable insight into the final and most difficult stretches of the trail. Without the generous assistance of these five individuals, my Oregon Trail adventure would have been greatly diminished. To them I offer my sincere gratitude.

As I biked along the trail I kept a daily journal. It's my journal entries that form the core of this book. After a brief introduction to the history of the Oregon Trail, each of the following chapters tells the story of a separate year. My day-to-day experiences are laid open before you. You'll visit the sites I visited. You'll meet the people I met. And gradually you'll come to appreciate, as I have done, the challenges faced by our ancestors 170 years ago. A plaque at the Great Platte River Road Archway Museum in Kearney, Nebraska, says it best: "The Cowards Never Started. The Weak Died On The Way. Only The Strong Arrived. They Were The Pioneers."

A Short History of a Long Trail

It's been called the largest voluntary migration in human history. In the three decades between 1840 and 1870 almost a half million people said goodbye to family and friends and headed west towards a new life. Most started from the middle of the country in states like Illinois and Indiana and Ohio. Some were looking for free land in Oregon, some for easy riches in the goldfields of California, and some for religious autonomy in Utah. Many of these pioneers also left home just for the adventure or because "everyone else was doing it." Restlessness has always been a defining American trait.

The Oregon Trail did not come about because of any individual or government. Nor did it suddenly appear in final form. It sprang from many different seeds, then evolved and matured through the years. Its spirit lives on in the descendants of those who first followed it. In fact, many people still follow it, intentionally or not.

Although the coastline of the Pacific Northwest had been explored by seafarers since the 1600s, little was known of the interior. Alexander Mackenzie, a Scottish explorer and fur trapper, made the first successful land crossing of North America north of Spanish territory in 1793. He struck the coast above Vancouver Island. Other trappers slowly followed but the first detailed view our young nation got of this region came from the writings of Lewis and Clark. Their Corps of Discovery set out in May 1804, and eighteen months later arrived at the mouth of the Columbia River. Except for the final stretch along the Columbia, Lewis and Clark's path stayed well north of what would become the Oregon Trail. When they returned in September 1806, they reported their findings to President Thomas Jefferson. Jefferson soon followed with a brief report to Congress. Before long the whole expedition was forgotten, at least by the general public.

But Jefferson never forgot. Word of the discoveries made by Lewis and Clark eventually passed from Jefferson to John Jacob Astor,

America's first multi-millionaire. Astor, a German-born immigrant to North America, had spent many years working with the fur trade in Canada. He invested his profits into real estate in New York City and made his fortune. The fur trade, however, still resonated within him. He wanted desperately to create his own company in the Pacific Northwest to compete with the British and the French. The knowledge acquired by the Corps of Discovery was just what Astor needed. He pitched his idea to Jefferson and won his support. In 1808, Astor formed the American Fur Trading Company and a subsidiary, the Pacific Fur Company.

Astor went to work organizing a two-pronged expedition to the mouth of the Columbia River. In 1810, an overland party departed for the northwest under the leadership of William Price Hunt. After leaving St. Louis, they spent the winter along the Missouri River just north of St. Joseph, Missouri. Moving on in the spring of 1811, they followed the Missouri River until they reached the mouth of the Grand River in today's South Dakota. Here, rather than following Lewis and Clarks' trail further north, they turned west. Hunt wanted to stay south to avoid the troublesome Blackfeet Indians. As the group entered the country that would later become Yellowstone National Park, they decided to try and float down the Snake River. This proved to be a disaster. After nine days they abandoned their boats and continued on foot. The route they blazed along the Snake River became an early link in the Oregon Trail chain. In February 1812, Hunt's overland expedition finally reached the mouth of the Columbia.

As Hunt made his way by land to the Pacific, the other half of Astor's plan was sailing around Cape Horn on the Tonquin. This ship, with its passengers and cargo, arrived at the Columbia in March 1811. The men immediately went to work building Fort Astoria. Farther up the coast, a few months later, and long before Hunt's arrival at the new fort, the Tonquin was attacked by Indians. Rather than surrendering it, the crew blew up the ship. This left the occupants of the new fort without a way to send their furs to market. It also made communication with John Jacob Astor all the more difficult.

With no easy way to get word to Astor about the Tonquin incident, it was decided to send a group back east with company dispatches and personal letters. In June 1812, Robert Stuart and six other men left Fort Astoria. In November they "discovered" South Pass in present day Wyoming. This pass through the Rocky Mountains was the key to the entire Oregon Trail, but like Lewis and Clark's discoveries before them, the discoveries made by the Astorians were also soon forgotten. America was now engaged in a second war with Great Britain.

The importance of South Pass to the development of the Oregon Trail can't be overstated. Migration westward was inevitable, of course, but without South Pass, it would have been delayed many years. It wasn't, as is often claimed, the only way for wagons to cross the Rocky Mountains; it was just the only practical way. The approach to South Pass, from either direction, had the three things necessary for easy passage: gentle grades, accessible water, and sufficient forage.

For two decades after South Pass was first crossed by the Astorians, its existence remained virtually unknown except to a handful of trappers including Jedediah Smith. In 1832, Captain Benjamin Bonneville, officially on a leave of absence from the U.S. Army, led an expedition of 100 men and 20 wagons over South Pass. This proved once and for all that wagons could indeed cross the Rockies.

In 1833, Hall Kelley set out for Oregon via New Orleans and Mexico. He had become enamored with Oregon since reading the accounts of Lewis and Clark and the Astorians. Without ever actually seeing Oregon, in the 1820s he began lobbying the Massachusetts Legislature and the U.S. Congress to promote the idea of settlement in the West. Now, he must have felt, it was time to see the land for himself. After arriving in California, he traveled north by horseback to Oregon in 1834. There he contracted malaria and was rescued by the Hudson's Bay Company (HBC). Once he recovered at Fort Vancouver, HBC promptly sent him on his way. He sailed to Hawaii and then back to his home in Boston. Although his stay in Oregon was short-lived, he continued to sing the praises of the land. His writings helped spur the missionary movement that soon followed.

Two years later, in 1836, a caravan of fur trappers traveled through South Pass accompanied by four Presbyterian missionaries. Among the missionaries were Narcissa Whitman and Eliza Spalding. They are often credited as the first white women to cross the pass but this is not completely true. Narcissa and Eliza traveled though South Pass (it's over twenty miles wide), they just didn't cross the traditional summit where markers were later placed. Instead, their group remained on the north side of the Sweetwater River and followed it northwest to its origin. They crossed the Continental Divide on a small ridge between the Sweetwater River and the Little Sandy River drainages. Still, the significance of Narcissa and Eliza's accomplishment is undeniable.

They settled the question as to whether the "fairer sex" could make such an arduous journey. If the West was to ever be populated in a meaningful way, it would have to be accessible to wagons *and* women.

So with a rough draft of the trail in place, and with the Rocky Mountains now conquered by wagons and women, all that remained to start the migration was a group of folks crazy enough to give it a try. Fortunately, the United States has never had a shortage of these people. First up to bat was the Western Emigration Society, organized in 1841 by John Bidwell and led by Captain John Bartleson. Their party consisted of 14 wagons and nearly 70 men, women, and children. Although most of the group had a working knowledge of wagons and livestock, they were clueless of the route. Their destination was California but all they really knew was it was west of Independence, Missouri. Fortune rarely smiles upon the unprepared but the Bidwell-Bartleson party got a lucky break. Another group of travelers was preparing to head out on the trail at about the same time. Six Jesuit missionaries, led by Father Pierre-Jean de Smet and guided by the famous mountain man Thomas "Broken Hand" Fitzpatrick, were going to Fort Hall, Idaho. They allowed the larger body of emigrants to tag along. Fitzpatrick, by the way, had earned his nickname due to his crippled left hand, the result of an earlier gun accident.

By the time the Western Emigration Society reached Soda Springs, Idaho, about half of their group had second thoughts. Bidwell and Bartleson, along with 32 others, including one woman and her young child, chose to continue to California. They brought nine wagons with them but all were eventually discarded. The land was simply too rough. They arrived in California with only what they could themselves physically carry. The defectors, meanwhile, chose to follow the Jesuits to Fort Hall. There they transferred their belongings to pack animals and continued on to Walla Walla, Washington. When they reached the Columbia River they boarded boats to complete their journey to the Willamette Valley. All arrived safely, though without their wagons.

The following year 1842, saw a second party of overland emigrants assembling in Independence. Slightly larger than the Bidwell-Bartleson effort, this group consisted of 105 people and 16 wagons. They were brought together by Elijah White. He expected to be chosen as their Captain but was challenged by, and nearly defeated by, Langsford Hastings. Factions within the party immediately formed and would be the distinguishing characteristic of their trek across the continent. Just beyond Fort Laramie, Wyoming, the party's original guide was replaced by Thomas Fitzpatrick. By chance, Fitzpatrick and mountain man Jim Bridger were headed east to Fort Laramie when they met the wagon train. Although many in the group balked at the high price Fitzpatrick was demanding, Elijah White recognized the value of experience and offered him the job. For the second time in two summers, "Broken Hand" Fitzpatrick found himself leading a caravan to Fort Hall. As in the previous summer, Elijah White's train abandoned their wagons at the fort. The commandant of Fort Hall, Richard Grant, drew detailed maps to the Columbia River but also told the emigrants that wagons would never make it through the Blue Mountains. Once again the final push to the Willamette Valley was completed on foot, with pack animals, and by boat.

The watershed year for the Oregon Trail was 1843. In March, a report of John C. Fremont's first expedition to the West was published in many eastern newspapers. "Oregon Fever" spread through the population at epidemic speed. Within a month people started streaming in to Independence. As the crowd grew, they moved to a staging area about twenty miles further west at Elm Grove (near present day Olathe, Kansas). On May 20th, the Oregon Emigrating Company was formed. Committees were created, a constitution was drawn up, a leader was elected, and a firm departure date was set. In all, on May 22nd, over a thousand people and two-hundred wagons left Elm Grove. It remains the largest single emigrant wagon train ever to roll west. Historians call it the "Great Migration."

It quickly became obvious that managing such a large group of independently minded people would be like herding the proverbial cats. Everyone wanted to be in charge but no one wanted to follow orders. Rifts were forming before the Great Migration had even cleared Kansas. Soon two main subgroups arose: a lead party of the quickest wagon travelers followed by the slower moving livestock herders. Additional splits occurred throughout the entire trip. In Nebraska, while crossing the South Platte River, the wagon train was joined by Marcus Whitman. Whitman was a trained physician who established a mission with his wife Narcissa near Walla Walla in 1836. His skills would come in handy for most of the remaining journey. Perhaps his greatest contribution to the Great Migration, however, was his staunch belief that wagons could make the trip all the way to the Columbia River. Dr. Whitman was now on his third crossing of the Oregon Trail. If anyone's judgment could be trusted, it was his. With Whitman's encouragement, segments of the Oregon Emigrating Company did indeed become the first train to successfully reach the Columbia with wagons in tow. The floodgate was now open.

For the next thirty years, the trail and the people who followed it continued to evolve. What began as a narrow path of footprints and wagon tracks became a highway of crisscrossing lanes. Each year new shortcuts and alternate routes would be tested. Some would last, others would be quickly abandoned. This is probably one of the hardest things for new students of the Oregon Trail to grasp. There was no single trail; there were only single strands of a much thicker rope. Likewise, there was no single type of pioneer. The first emigrants tended to be farmers with their families. Most were what we would call today "middle class." It wasn't cheap to buy wagons and oxen and supplies for a five month journey. The poor couldn't afford it, and the rich generally had no reason to head west. In 1847, a different kind of pioneer appeared on the scene. These were religious pilgrims, mostly recent converts focused on gathering at a new paradise in Utah. Like the other pioneers, they tended to be families. Many had just stepped off their ships in America from poor European backgrounds. In fact, some were so poor they couldn't even afford the traditional covered wagons. Beginning in 1856 many Mormons resorted to loading their possessions onto handcarts and pushing them all the way to the Salt Lake Basin.

And then everything changed. In 1848, with the discovery of gold in California, the nature of trail travel shifted dramatically. Rather than families who were intent on making a new, permanent home in the West, the gold seekers were mainly young, single men. Most hoped to strike it rich as fast as possible in the goldfields and then return east with their newfound wealth. What they had in ambition, they often lacked in the skills necessary for making an extended trail crossing. Gradually though, as gold fever subsided, the crowds on the trail reverted to tamer compositions.

It's difficult to pinpoint exactly when the Oregon Trail began. Was it in 1841 with the Bidwell-Bartleson party? Or was it earlier, in 1812, when the Astorians followed most of the eventual route from Oregon to St. Louis? Most historians consider 1843 as the start of the "classical period" of the Oregon Trail. After all, the Great Migration was the first group to make it all the way to the Columbia River with their wagons. What would the Oregon Trail be without covered wagons?

The end of the trail is more easily defined. With the driving of the Golden Spike in 1869, five months of hardship crossing the continent were no longer necessary. By riding the iron horse, the west coast was only a week away. Occasional solitary wagons were seen on the trail as late as 1912 but the days of the organized wagon train were over.

As the United States moved into the twentieth century, the physical traces of the Oregon Trail were already beginning to fade. Large tracts of land were being fenced. Grazing herds and sharpened plows were erasing the wagon ruts. Even lakes, formed by an ever increasing number of man-made dams, were covering the trail. If not for the preservation efforts began by one man, much of the trail we see today would be gone.

Ezra Meeker was born in Huntsville, Ohio on December 29, 1830. As a young man, he moved to Indiana, where he met his wife Eliza. They decided they wanted to be farmers on their own land. At that time land was still cheap in Iowa, so in October 1851 they headed west. One brutal Iowa winter was all it took to convince Ezra that Iowa was not the place for him. As he later wrote in 1912, "I vowed then and there that I did not like the Iowa climate, and the Oregon fever was visibly quickened." In April 1852, Ezra and his young wife and their one-month-old son set out from Iowa with a few relatives and friends. The number of pioneers traveling on the Oregon Trail that year was so high that the Meekers felt no need to join an organized train. According to Ezra, the white canopies of wagons could always be seen in front of and behind their own small party.

Five months later, most of the Meekers arrived safely in Oregon Territory. Ezra's mother, Phoebe, was the exception. She had succumbed to cholera as the party rolled into Wyoming. Ezra settled in the area of present day Puyallup, Washington, and over the next 50 years became a successful farmer, businessman, and civic leader. As he entered the eighth decade of his life, however, his adventures were far from over. He began to notice that many of his pioneer friends were dying, and most of their stories were dying with them. He also recognized that vast stretches of the Oregon Trail were being lost to development.

In 1906, at the age of 75, he began to retrace his original trek along the trail with a wagon and two oxen. One of his goals was to promote a cross-country highway that would follow the route the original trail. This trip took two years. Along the way he stop in each town and encourage the local residents to erec to commemorate the Oregon Trail and its pioneers. Sometimes the monuments would be financed, constructed, erected, and dedicated all in the period of a few days. At other times, the seeds of the project would be planted, and the fruit coming to bear within a year or two. According to Meeker, many of the monuments were paid for with the "dimes and half-dimes" of local school children. Surviving two trips along the Oregon Trail was still not enough for Ezra. In 1910 he traveled the entire route again by wagon. Like before, he promoted the idea of marking and preserving the trail at numerous public gatherings.

Ezra lived in a remarkable time in history. During his lifetime he saw the end of the horse and buggy days and the arrival of the industrial age. In 1916 he once again followed the trail by automobile. In 1924 Ezra Meeker made his final trip along the Oregon Trail. You can't say he was "on the trail" this time, though. At the age of 94 he flew as a passenger above the trail in an open cockpit biplane. "What changes time has wrought" he observed. Ezra died four years later in 1928.

Following Ezra's death, the challenge of preserving the trail fell mainly to private organizations. Local historic societies and civic groups, even the Boy Scouts, began to place markers at various sites. The efforts were rarely coordinated, but each contributed in part to keeping the trail visible. In Nebraska, for example, a number of granite markers were placed along the route in 1912. It was many more years, however, before a national effort was put into motion to save what was left.

The National Parks and Recreation Act of 1978 authorized the designation of "National Historic Trails." Each trail considered for such a designation has to be approved by an Act of Congress. The Oregon Trail was the first. Eighteen additional trails have since joined the list, the last being added in 2009. From a federal standpoint, management of the Oregon National Historical Trail falls to the National Park Service (NPS). They coordinate the efforts of other agencies such as the Bureau of Land Management (BLM) and the

The BLM has done an especially good job retive centers in Casper, Wyoming, and Baker

ts have also taken steps to preserve individual orders. Rock Creek State Historic Site in and the Guernsey Ruts in Wyoming, and ate Park in Idaho are great examples. Local governments, too, have done their part. They often form alliances with non-profit organizations to help protect and promote the trail within their own communities. In Pocatello, Idaho, a replica of Fort Hall sits in a town park. In Oregon City, Oregon, the End of the Oregon Trail Interpretive Center is operated in partnership with several local tourism bureaus. Towns all along the trail have learned that historic preservation attracts tourists. Everyone benefits.

Private landowners are increasingly involved with trail preservation. Some simply allow trail enthusiasts to cross their land without having to ask first. Others have gone so far as to build walkways or monuments at their own expense to help keep the trail alive. If not for the efforts of so many different groups and individuals, the Oregon Trail would slowly fade back into the landscape. Along with it, many chapters of our American narrative would also be erased forever.

Oregon Trail monument on Courthouse Square, Independence, Missouri. This is the "official" start of the Oregon Trail. *39.092481, -94.416462*

Gardner Junction, near Gardner, Kansas. At this spot, the Oregon Trail and Santa Fe Trail split. *38.796433, -94.961717*

Out Onto the Prairie
2012

My first year riding along the Oregon Trail was a series of learning events. When traveling on a bicycle, a few ounces here and there don't matter. A few pounds here and there add up quickly. I made the same mistake a lot of the early pioneers made: I overloaded the wagon. It's one thing to pull a bicycle trailer 50 miles across the flat land of southern Louisiana. It's something entirely different to drag it up and down the rolling hills of northeastern Kansas. Soon after "jumping off" onto the prairie, many emigrants were forced to unload family heirlooms from their wagons. Grandma's china or the prized armoire would be of little use if your oxen died trying to haul it to Oregon. The trail between Independence and Kearney was littered with the trappings of civilized life. Luckily, my wagon was much smaller. I didn't have to jettison anything but I did pay a price for some of the "luxuries" I brought with me.

I also learned something about the wind. Near the Gulf Coast in the spring and summer the wind is usually light and variable from the southeast. On the open prairies of the Midwest the wind is usually from the west. This meant I was almost always pedaling into a headwind. I paid a price for that also.

In the middle of the nineteenth century the land around Independence was mostly wooded or cultivated. Not much grassland was left by that time. But as the wagons left Missouri, they entered a landscape still dominated by tall grass prairie. The sudden change reinforced the fact that they were leaving the familiar behind. I had no sense of this. Today, Independence is a suburb of Kansas City. Except for the terrain, Missouri looked identical to Kansas. I saw the same strip malls and chain stores that can be found in any sizable city these days.

Moving away from Kansas City, I rolled into an area of farms and the small towns that grew to support them. It wasn't until a decade after the first travelers on the Oregon Trail passed that others were free to stop and settle in Kansas and Nebraska. The change wasn't immediate but slowly this area was transformed into America's Breadbasket. Even now the landscape is evolving. The family farms of the past century are being collected into large, corporate-owned agricultural enterprises. The surrounding towns are fading away. So many of the communities I rode through in 2012 were only ghosts of their former selves. As young people grow up they have to move away to find work. As the older residents pass on, their homes stay vacant and decay. The schools consolidate with nearby towns and hold on as long as they can. In rural America, schools are the heart of a community. When they close, the town slowly withers away. I saw it again and again. This, I learned, is the current state of the tall grass prairie and the communities planted upon it.

Friday, May 18ᵗʰ - Arrival at Independence, MO

Since my oldest son had finished his college finals a few days earlier, he drove me to the Amtrak station in Hammond, Louisiana. This is the closest train station to home. While I waited to catch the City of New Orleans northbound, I admired the architecture of the old building. The station master said it was constructed in 1913, and Amtrak took it over in 2000. I noticed on the walls, that every three feet or so a thin wooden strip was embedded between the bricks. He explained that once the brick work was finished, chicken wire would be stapled to the wooden strips and then plaster applied and painted. This was a common technique in the days before sheetrock. Another passenger, an elderly man, said when he was a kid he used to get paid a penny a piece to clean the plaster off of old bricks so they could be used again. Recycling is nothing new.

I boarded the City of New Orleans at 3:00 p.m. This is Amtrak's daily passenger train that runs between New Orleans and Chicago. If you've aged properly, you may also remember that Arlo Guthrie made this train semi-famous in song. Twelve hours later, and with little sleep, I arrived at Carbondale, Illinois. Travel on Amtrak is great if you happen to be going where they want to go. Otherwise, it's a pretty pathetic national rail system. My train was heading to Chicago but I needed to go to Independence by way of St. Louis. So at 3:15 a.m., I transferred to an Amtrak shuttle bus to carry me to the next stop.

I arrived at the Gateway Station in St. Louis at 6:00 a.m. It's a combination bus and train station. They had a small deli in the terminal but it was certainly nothing to write home about. Breakfast consisted of a honeybun and orange juice. After a three hour layover I continued west on Amtrak's Missouri River Runner. Unlike the previous train, this train was completely packed with passengers. I talked with another cyclist who was on his way to ride the Katy Trail, Missouri's famous cross-state bicycle path. He hoped to complete the 300 miles in three days.

My train rolled into Independence right on time at 2:20 p.m. I was met at the station by my host, Bennie. He owned the Three Trails Inn where I had reservations for the next two nights. The inn was built in 1889 and Bennie and his wife had been operating it as a bed and breakfast for the past two years. After a shower and a nap I walked down to Courthouse Square. Along the way I passed a number of stately old Victorian homes including the Harry Truman house. Surrounding the square are many small shops and eateries. I focused on the Rheinland, a German restaurant that turned out to be wunderbar. My home state of Louisiana is known for its great food, but German restaurants are almost non-existent. The Rheinland was a real treat for me. I had the *jaegerschnitsel* and *spaezle* and washed it down with a huge frosty mug of dark beer (never trust beer you can see through). I definitely did my part that evening to support America's obesity epidemic.

After waddling back to the Three Trails Inn, I began the task of unpacking and reassembling my bike. I had previously shipped the bike and all of my gear to the inn by FedEx. With the ridiculous baggage fees charged by the airlines and Amtrak these days, it costs no more to ship the equipment than to carry it with you. Plus, you don't have to drag it though the terminals. As I unpacked the boxes, I was happy to find all the pieces intact. An hour later everything was back together with no parts left over. That's always a good sign.

Saturday, May 19th - Around Independence, MO - 25 miles

Bennie cooked up a batch of homemade waffles so I had a full tank of fuel to start my exploration of Independence. First I rode north to the Wayne City Overlook. From this point you can look down to the Missouri River and the site of the old Independence Landing. During the earliest days of travel on the Oregon Trail most emigrants arrived at Independence by steamboat from St. Louis. They disembarked at Independence Landing and made their way up the steep bluff towards the present overlook. From here they followed a ridge down to Courthouse Square. Today Wayne City Road and North River Boulevard follow roughly the same path. When I arrived at Wayne City Road, however, I found a locked gate. A nearby sign read "LaFarge – Private Property – No Trespassing." I called the number on the sign but no one answered. I knew the overlook wasn't more than a hundred yards beyond the gate, so I slipped around it. I figured I could be in and out before any security guys could finish their donuts. I was right; mission accomplished.

From the overlook, I rode downriver to LaBenite Park. It's the only place I could find to perform the "dipping of the wheel" ritual to appease the cycling gods. Cross country cyclists traditionally dip a wheel into the ocean before they start their ride, and dip it in the other ocean when they finish. In the 1840s the Missouri River was figuratively the west coast of the United States so I figured that would count. Then I biked back to Independence and visited some of the historic sites near Courthouse Square. The square is dominated appropriately enough by the Jackson County courthouse. On the west side of the courthouse is a monument dedicated to the Oregon Trail pioneers. This monument is the official start of the trail.

My next stop was the National Frontier Trails Museum. It's not a bad museum but many of the displays are dated. The initial movie you see when you arrive was produced in 1990. The whole place needs a facelift. Just south of the museum is the Bingham-Waggoner Estate. It was built after the days of the Oregon Trail but the land where it sits was a popular staging area for wagons heading out first on the Santa Fe Trail and then later on the Oregon Trail. A small creek runs along the south side of the property. As wagons made their way across the creek and up the other side, they left ruts in the ground. These ruts, more correctly called swales, are still visible today. They're very faint here, but at other places they're more obvious.

Finally, after I had finished touring the sites around Independence Square, I rode a few miles west to the Mount Washington Cemetery. Here I made a pilgrimage to the grave of the famed mountain man, trapper, explorer, teller of tall tales, and all-around adventurer, Jim Bridger. If he actually did half the stuff he's credited with, it's still a hundred times more than most men will ever do. He is probably best known for establishing Fort Bridger in southwestern Wyoming. He also supposedly gave Brigham Young directions to find the Great Salt Lake in Utah. According to legend, when Young told Bridger of his plans to create a new paradise in the Salt Lake Basin, Bridger told him he'd give him a thousand dollars for the first bushel of corn produced. There's no word if he ever paid up.

Sunday, May 20ᵗʰ - Independence, MO, to Gardner Junction, KS - 52 miles

I hit the trail at 9:00 a.m. Of all my planned days of riding, I worried about this one the most. Aside from the normal first day jitters, the thought of riding 50 miles in city traffic was not very appealing. My hope was that by leaving on a Sunday morning the roads would be a little less congested. That seemed to be the case. The route first took me south to Santa Fe Park. Within the park, faint swales of an untold number of wagons are still visible and marked. I continued south, then southwest through Raytown, and on to the Manchester Ruts. These ruts are a bit more obvious and are located at the intersection of Manchester Road and East 85ᵗʰ Street. From here the original trail headed southwest, however, I turned west onto Bannister Road with the intention of hitting Blue River Road and following it south to Blue River Crossing. That was where the pioneers made their first actual river crossing. Less than a mile down Blue River Road, though, I encountered my first obstacle. Barricades had been placed on the road. Recent spring rains washed out sections of the road and made it impassable. I was forced to detour back to Bannister Road and follow the west side of the Blue River south.

I crossed into Kansas at the intersection of Santa Fe Trail and State Line Road. Near this intersection was once located the village of New Santa Fe. Until it was abandoned during the Bleeding Kansas days it was the last supply point for Oregon Trail travelers before they left the United States. Once they crossed the state line, they were in Indian country. United States laws were rarely, if ever, enforced even if they did exist on paper. Most of the first wagon trains adopted charters in which the signers would agree to certain rules while on the trip. Pioneer journals are full of descriptions of frontier justice, including executions, being doled out to the noncompliant.

It's odd how the terrain altered just by crossing the Blue River. On a bicycle you're much more aware of these changes than when driving a car. While on the Missouri side, I climbed hill after hill. Once I rode into Kansas, though, the land flattened out a bit. I continued stair-stepping west and south until I came to Lone Elm Park. It was here that many wagon trains spent their first night on foreign soil. Pioneers called it the Lone Elm campground for reasons that don't seem so obvious today. In the 1840s, most of the surrounding land was tall grass prairie. A solitary tree here or there was considered a major landmark. It's hard to imagine such an environment when today all you see are cookie cutter subdivisions and trees. Lone Elm Park has some hiking trails, but mainly it's covered with ball fields. There are also excellent interpretive panels which explain the important history of the area. It was mid-afternoon when I arrived at Lone Elm so I took advantage of a nice pavilion to rest and enjoy some peace and quiet in the shade. The peace didn't last long, though, as I was soon surrounded by a couple dozen 2nd grade soccer players. That was my cue to move on.

Just south of the town of Gardner is a nice interpretive site called Gardner Junction. It's here where the Santa Fe Trail and the Oregon Trail split. The Santa Fe Trail was mainly a commercial trail that continued across southern Kansas and into Colorado and New Mexico. It was blazed in the 1820s but was never used much by emigrants. The terrain beyond Santa Fe was too broken for wagons. At the split, there once was a sign that simply pointed right and said "Road to Oregon." Remember, it was not called the Oregon Trail during emigration days. It was called the Oregon Road.

Today the Gardner Junction Historic Site has a small pavilion and a paved walking trail with benches. The grounds have been landscaped with native grasses and other plants to show what the area would have looked like 170 years ago. Interpretive panels also tell the story of the site. Overnight camping is usually not allowed since there are no restrooms. Prior to starting my trip, however, I contacted the town of Gardner and got permission to spend the night. I planned to use the nearby woods as needed but a porta-potty had been conveniently placed across the street by railroad construction crews. It worked out perfectly for me.

Monday, May 21st - Gardner Junction, KS, to Topeka, KS - 59 miles

Note to self: Avoid camping next to railroad tracks. I pitched my tent under the pavilion at Gardner Junction. Even though I had permission to camp there, I waited until almost dark to set up. Touring cyclists call this "stealth camping." Although it usually means setting up on private land or public land where you're not supposed to be, in my case I just wanted to avoid any undue attention from drivers on the nearby highway. I didn't sleep as well as I had hoped. Between the noise of passing freight trains every fifteen minutes, and muscle cramps in my legs, I was tossing and turning all night. When I ride at home, I don't lose moisture as fast because of the humidity. Typically, I drink about three bottles of water on a daylong ride. On the prior day's ride, however, I went through eight bottles and still ended up with leg cramps. To prevent this from happening again, I decided to alternate plain water with water mixed with mineral tablets. It helped.

I left Gardner Junction at 7:00 a.m. All in all it was a pleasant day of riding. I learned that northeastern Kansas does indeed have hills, though, but not as many as Missouri. I only had two sites on my list of things to see today. The first was Blue Mound. As hills go, Blue Mound doesn't look that impressive. It's covered by trees today, but in the 1840s it was blanketed with the same tall grass as the surrounding prairie. It stood out as the first real landmark the emigrants encountered on their trip. Many travelers, including John C. Fremont and Kit Carson, scaled its peak for no other reason than to sightsee.

Blue Mound. Located near Lawrence, Kansas, this small hill was the first significant landmark the pioneers saw after leaving Missouri. *38.904468, -95.182607*

Just south of Lawrence, I came to my second stop of the day. The Wakarusa River runs along the southern edge of town and at Wakarusa Crossing the wagon trains made their second fording of a river. Unlike the Blue River back near Independence, the Wakarusa River had steep, rocky banks that made the crossing difficult. By Louisiana standards it looks no wider than a big ditch, but many pioneers ended their journey here. Along the trail, drowning was a leading cause of death. In fact, the three most common causes of accidental death among the emigrants were drowning, firearms mishaps, and being rolled over by a wagon wheel.

I rode into Lawrence right at lunchtime. I was starving and really low on energy. Cyclists call this "bonking." For whatever reason, I had neglected to eat anything before starting my day. I had plenty of food in my panniers. I was just too lazy to dig it out and too anxious to get on the road. I found a pasta place and did some serious carb-loading. The manager noticed my bike and asked me all about my trip. It's amazing how many people say they would like to do an adventure but so few ever start. As I was leaving the restaurant he gave me two freshly baked double chocolate cookies for energy. They worked very well.

I made an unplanned stop in Lawrence at the Sunflower Bike Shop. I needed to stock up on mineral tablets for my water bottles and I knew that bike shops usually carry the brand I like. Camelbak Elixir tablets are like powdered Gatorade without all the sugar. I bought a couple of packs and was soon on my way.

I made it into Topeka at around 4:00 p.m. and pitched my tent in a real campground. Shawnee Lake Park is a county park with camping, fishing, swimming, and a bike path that circles around the lake. The path looked nice but I figured I'd ridden enough for one day. When I went to take a shower I discovered they only had cold water. It was a shock at first but I endured. Shaving, however, was another thing entirely. Also, since I only carried two sets of riding clothes with me, I had to do laundry every other night. I was able use the park's laundry room before going to sleep.

Tuesday, May 22nd – Topeka, KS, to Westmoreland, KS – 62 miles

I was a bit nervous about riding through Topeka during the morning rush but it turned out to be easier than expected. After the first five miles I dropped from the bluffs into the Kansas River valley and had flat roads for the next 35 miles. In Topeka I crossed the Kansas River on the Topeka Avenue Bridge. This bridge is just upstream from the site of the original pioneer crossing. In 1842, the Papin brothers built a ferry at the site, but many travelers were either unable or unwilling to pay the toll. Like many later ferries on the Oregon Trail, the tolls varied with the conditions of the water. In times of swift current, the Papins' tolls could exceed $1.00 per wagon. Even if the tolls were paid, safe crossings were not guaranteed. Local Indians often fished people and property from the river when wagons flipped.

In North Topeka I turned west on U.S Highway 24 towards the town of Silverlake. I passed a lot of huge grain elevators along the way. What caught my attention were the signs that read, "Remote control locomotives operate in this area. Locomotive cabs may be unoccupied." It just struck me as a bad idea. I continued through the town of Rossville and made it into St. Marys for lunch. St. Marys' claim to fame is the St. Mary's Academy. Something like a third of the town's residents are employed there. I grabbed lunch at the B&B Café. The place is so local they don't even bother with a sign. The townspeople just know it's there. I got directions to the place from a native but still missed it on the first try. I found it on my second attempt and it was worth the effort.

Leaving town, I followed Oregon Trail Road. It's a gravel road that's built directly on top of the original trail. About four miles west of town I came to Oregon Trail Park. Three guys were sitting under the pavilion playing cards so I sat and joined them for a few minutes. Charlie, John, and Earl filled me in on all the local history. In the park is an old silo that has been painted with Oregon Trail scenes. By chance I met Cynthia. She's the local artist who originally painted the silo 16 years earlier. She said she repaints it every other year. The local power company loans her a bucket truck so she can get to the upper reaches of the silo.

After I left Oregon Trail Park, I continued west to Vieux Crossing. Louis Vieux built a bridge here across the Vermillion River in the 1850s. On a good day, he claimed, he could make over $300.00 in tolls. Before the bridge, in 1849, a wagon train camped near the crossing and was stricken by Asiatic cholera. During this time cholera took more lives than any other single cause. In this wagon train alone nearly 50 people died in a matter of days. They were buried along the east side of the river. A short hike to the north of the road leads to a

Vieux Crossing. The pavilion protects what little remains of the Vieux Elm. In the foreground are the graves of seven unidentified soldiers killed during the Indian Wars. *39.256431, -96.249813*

small cemetery. Only three headstones remain and only one of those is still legible. It reads, "T.S. Prather, 1849."

On the west bank of the river are the remains of the Vieux Elm. That tree witnessed the westward migration firsthand and in 1979 was named the U.S. Champion Elm. A few years later vandals blew it up with a pipe bomb. The county placed a fence around the burnt stump and put a roof over it but it's just a matter of time before everything rots away. Near the pavilion are also seven grave markers for unidentified soldiers who died here during the Indian wars.

I had planned to camp at Vieux Crossing but a really strong south wind convinced me to move on. I knew I'd soon be turning north so it would have been sinful to squander a good tailwind. I rode another 14 miles to Westmoreland. Just before coming into town I stopped at the roadside historic park at Scott Springs. This was a popular watering hole and campground for the pioneers. A large covered wagon and oxen statue, along with several interpretive signs, tell the story of Scott Springs. A short paved trail leads from the park into town.

Over the previous six months, I had been e-mailing back and

forth with Nola, a member of the Rock Creek Historical Society in Westmoreland. She met me at the society's museum and gave me the grand tour of the place. Later we drove around town and she pointed out all the historic sites. One particularly interesting place was a hand-dug water well constructed in 1916. It measured 29 feet in diameter. A few years earlier, when the town decided to restore it, they had to remove over a dozen junked cars from the water. Nola invited me to spend the night at her and her husband Larry's home. How could I refuse such a kind offer? Larry grilled some burgers and we had a delicious dinner. I was able to get cleaned up, do some laundry, and sleep in a real bed. This was small town hospitality at its best.

Wednesday, May 23rd - Westmoreland, KS, to Alcove Spring, KS - 45 miles

At 7:30 a.m. I said goodbye to my hosts Nola and Larry and started north from Westmoreland. The ride that day was interesting because of the very high winds: 25 mph from the south and 40 mph gusts. With a great tailwind I was pushed right along for the first 16

Alcove Spring. Named by a member of the Donner Party in 1846, this site has been called the most important Oregon Trail site in Kansas. *39.749821, -96.678963*

29

miles. Then I turned west and quickly learned how far you have to lean a bike over to keep it going straight with 40 mph crosswinds. Soon I came to my first point of interest for the day: the Lower Crossing of the Black Vermillion River. Near this spot in 1844, an ill member of the "Company of Catholics,"– a group of 20 parishioners led by an unnamed Jesuit priest – died and was buried on the ridge west of the river. Guided by famed mountain man Andrew Sublette, they were traveling from St. Louis to Fort Laramie, Wyoming. Hoping the drier western climate would restore their health, three more passed away before ever leaving Kansas. The first, James Marshall, died here on June 27th. Five years later another emigrant observed that the simple wooden cross was still in place and formed a "magnificent silhouette" against the sunset. Sadly, his grave has now been lost.

I arrived in the town of Blue Rapids at noon. Taking my cue from the pioneers I decided to layover for a few hours until it started to cool down. Along with the unusually high winds (even by Kansas standards) the temperatures were way above average, approaching 85°F by midday. I had lunch at the Blue Valley Café. The café had been open for four years and the owner cooked everything from scratch. I indulged in a plate of homemade lasagna. It was excellent! After about an hour in the café I walked next door to the library. I charged my tablet and cell phone and soaked up the air conditioning. Lynn, the librarian, told me she had traveled throughout Europe in the past, staying in hostels along the way. Her favorite place was Istanbul. Her son, like me, was an Air Force Reservist. Finally, I wandered over to the Blue Rapids Museum. They were preparing for a reunion of graduates from Blue Rapids High School, that closed in 1962.

At 4:00 p.m. I left Blue Rapids and rode the last eight miles to Alcove Spring. Alcove Spring has been called the most historically significant Oregon Trail site in Kansas. Long before the Oregon Trail, Indians and trappers and explorers camped at the site because of the clear, cold water rushing out of the ground. In 1846, while the ill-fated Donner Party camped here, one of the men carved "Alcove Spring" into the rock ledge above the water. The name stuck. James Reed, another key player in the upcoming tragedy, also carved his name into the rock. His elderly mother-in-law, Sarah Keyes, died and was buried here. The exact location of her grave remains a mystery. Supposedly, there was also a Mormon cholera cemetery in the area but its location has also been forgotten.

Camping at Alcove Spring is not normally allowed but I had

obtained permission from the Alcove Spring Preservation Association to spend the night. I found a nice clearing and pitched my tent. There are no restrooms at the site but plenty of woods. Boardwalks and interpretive signs have been installed throughout the park. A short climb up a hill to the north provides a great view of the Big Blue River. After heavy spring thunderstorms wagon trains would often spend days here waiting for the swollen waters of the Big Blue to recede.

Thursday, May 24th - Alcove Spring, KS, to Hanover, KS - 24 miles

I didn't sleep as well as I hoped during the night. The evening started off peaceful enough, but by 11:00 p.m. I started seeing the flashes of distant lightning in the western sky. I checked the AccuWeather radar on my tablet and, sure enough, there was a thin band of yellows and reds coming my way. Knowing what thunderstorms are capable of this time of year in Kansas, I couldn't help but start running through possible escape options in my mind. Many pioneers wrote of similar fears. Sudden hail storms could kill, or at the very least, stampede

Hollenberg Station. The only original Pony Express Station still standing on its original site. *39.900933, -96.843821*

the livestock. The emigrants were especially vulnerable to lightning strikes on the open prairie. Worst of all were the tornados that plague the Midwest in spring and early summer. At least the pioneers could duck under their wagons for some shelter. A nylon tent provides little protection. Luckily for me, the storms veered off to the north. I eventually went back to sleep. Then around 4:00 a.m. I was awakened by a mixed chorus of barred owls and whip-poor-wills. This continued until sunrise.

As was becoming routine by now, I rode away from camp at 7:00 a.m. I biked about seven miles along a dirt road to the town of Marysville. As I rode, I passed many small farms situated in the valley of the Big Blue River. Some people may find the scent of hay and cattle in the morning offensive, but not me. Of all the senses, smell evokes the strongest and most immediate emotions. Certain smells have a way of transcending time and space. For me, the wafting aroma of barnyards instantly stirred childhood memories of my grandfather's farm in Nebraska. Both farm and farmer are now long gone.

I had been told of a local café in Marysville that served a great breakfast so while passing through town I stopped at the Wagon Wheel Café to judge for myself. I wasn't disappointed. The delicious western omelet and homemade hash browns really hit the spot. Only a short ride was planned for the day so there was no rush to leave. Marysville sits along the old military road that connected St. Joseph with the main Oregon Trail. The original trail passed just west of town. When St. Joseph became the preferred starting point for Oregon Trail travelers, the military road became their chosen route. In 1860 the road was also the primary route of the Pony Express. A nearby stone barn used by the Pony Express now contains a museum but I was too early to visit. A small park and reconstructed ferry are located on the banks of the Big Blue west of town.

The one historic site I visited on my ride to Hanover was the Hollenberg Pony Express Station. It's the only station that still stands on its original site. The station was built in 1858 as a ranch by Gerat Hollenberg. By that time most of the emigrant travel had shifted to "jumping off" points even further north than St. Joseph. Hollenberg's ranch was located right beside the original trail and he made substantial profits supplying the commercial traffic and stage lines that still used the route. In 1860, he was contracted to provide services to the newly formed Pony Express.

If you're not familiar with the Pony Express, it was an expedited mail service that promised delivery of a letter from St. Joseph, Missouri, to San Francisco, California, in the amazing time of only ten days. The whole venture lasted only 18 months, from the spring of 1860 to the autumn of 1861. In that short time, the Pony Express earned a lasting place in American history, but never a profit. Many sub-contractors like Hollenberg lost a fortune when the Pony Express went belly-up. The original cost to send a ½ ounce letter from St. Joseph to San Francisco was $5.00. In modern terms that would be almost $85.00. As the last wires of the first transcontinental telegraph were connected in 1861, the Pony Express immediately became obsolete.

I spent an hour wandering around the Hollenberg Station. I had hoped to get permission to camp on the grounds but no such luck this time. Katherine, the education coordinator for the museum, contacted the Town of Hanover on my behalf. I was put in touch with a local businessman, Joey, who opened the town's community center for me. The center had a roof, electricity, and showers. It was perfect; a nice finish to a short day.

Friday, May 25th - Hanover, KS, to Fairbury, NE - 39 miles

I had a peaceful afternoon and a restful evening at the Hanover Community Center. The road north out of Hanover had been recently repaved and was like riding on glass. When I crossed into Nebraska eight miles later the pavement got worse but still not too bad. Three miles further, I turned from north to west. What had been a quartering headwind from the northeast now became a tailwind. The next 14 miles flew by. Turning north again I soon arrived at Rock Creek Station State Historic Site.

Like Hollenberg Station, Rock Creek Station was built after most of the emigration had moved farther north. The station itself was established in 1857 on the west side of Rock Creek. Its main purpose was to supply the freight wagons and stagecoaches that passed along the trail. In 1859, David McCanles bought the station, made improvements, and built an accompanying station on the east bank of the creek. Rock Creek was an especially difficult creek to ford so McCanles built a toll bridge and charged between ten and fifty cents per wagon to cross. This would have been the end of the story had it not been for something that occurred there in July, 1861. McCanles had recently sold the property on the west side of the creek but stopped by to discuss a late payment with the new owner. An employee of the new owner, James Butler Hickok, fired a shot from behind a curtain and killed David McCanles. This was Wild Bill Hickok's first murder.

It was easy to spend several hours at Rock Creek Station. Paved walking trails, numerous reconstructed buildings, a fine museum, and some very impressive swales made my visit there go quickly. In time though I resumed my ride to Fairbury. In the center of Fairbury is the Jefferson County courthouse. Surrounding the courthouse is a town square with the usual shops and eateries. I planted myself into Jalisco's, a family owned Mexican restaurant that turned out to have fantastic fajitas. As I was walking out of Jalisco's I met a couple named Kris and Bryce. They owned a nearby ranch and were avid cyclists themselves. Each year they participate in the annual Bike Ride Across Nebraska (BRAN). They explained how BRAN brings the small rural communities together. At the end of each day, towns host the riders in their park. Civic and church groups cook meals, provide entertainment, and do their best to promote their home towns. The route changes every year so different communities can get involved. This also gives the riders a chance to experience new areas of the state.

On the southwest edge of Fairbury is Crystal Springs Park. It has a small community fishing lake and campground. As I rode in, I was surprised by the large crowds. Then I remembered this was the start of the long Memorial Day weekend.

Saturday, May 26th - Fairbury, NE, to Hebron, NE - 38 miles

I knew this day's ride would be rough. The forecast was predicting 25-30 mph southwest winds with near record heat. I had every intention of leaving camp by 6:00 a.m. but of course that didn't happen. As usual, it was closer to 7:00 a.m. While passing through Fairbury, I bought two extra bottles of water and stashed them in my bags. I also made sure to top off the three bottles I usually carried on the bike. This turned out to be a wise decision.

My first stop in the morning was at the grave of George Winslow. It's been estimated that between 25,000 and 30,000 people died along the Oregon Trail. That works out to an average of one grave every 500 feet. Very few of those graves have ever been found. In many cases the graves were purposely hidden or disguised to prevent animals or Indians from digging them up. In other cases, sandstone or wooden markers simply turned to dust. What makes Winslow's grave so unique is that we actually have documents that describe his death and burial. We also have personal letters from him to his wife.

In April 1849, George left his home in Boston and headed for the goldfields of California. He was traveling with a group of 24 other men of the Boston-Newton Joint Stock Association. Near the end of May he became ill with cholera. After resting for three days he appeared to be recovering. On June 6th, as his party crossed into Nebraska, they were hit by a severe thunderstorm. Being soaked with rain may have caused a relapse. George Winslow died on June 8th. He was 25. His grave is on private land but the public is welcomed to visit. Several other unmarked graves are close by.

In one of George's letters to his wife he said that he was sleeping very well. He added that his bedding had a slow leak and each morning he found himself "planted flatly on solid ground." This saved him the trouble of "squeezing out the atmosphere" before rolling his bed up. He said this so matter-of-factly that the use of air mattresses by pioneers must have been commonplace. Surprisingly, I've never seen any other mention of this.

I continued north for a couple more miles, then turned west. As I did, the full force of the wind and heat hit me. Combined with the loose sand and gravel on the road, my pace slowed to a crawl. With five miles left to ride, I was down to only two bottles of water. By luck, a local farmer had seen me on the road earlier. As I passed his house he came out to greet me. His name was Bob and he also was a history buff. We were soon joined by his son Jared. Bob told me of the time back in 1993, during the 150th anniversary of the Oregon Trail, when a wagon train of re-enactors rode in front of his home. A bee got under one of the horse's saddles. It bolted and ran through Bob's yard, almost smashing through his front picture window and into the room where his three year old daughter was sleeping. Fortunately, the horse was quickly grabbed and the wagon train moved on. Bob also showed me a mural his mother created back in 1993 for the anniversary. She carved it out of red bricks made in nearby Endicot, Nebraska. He proudly displays it in his front yard.

I filled my bottles with cold water from Bob's well then biked on to Hebron. These may have been the hardest five miles I've ever ridden. By the time I slithered into the local Subway it was 12:30 p.m. and 98°F. I was whipped! My plan was to camp in Hebron's Riverside Park. At nearly 100°F, though, it just didn't seem like fun. Hebron has three motels and you would think it would be easy to find a room. Not true. It was the Memorial Day weekend and the annual Hebron High

A replica of the toll bridge crossing Rock Creek at Rock Creek Station State Historical Park, Nebraska. *40.113167, -97.060190*

The grave of pioneer George Winslow is well marked in the middle of a farmer's field north of Fairbury, Nebraska. *40.207618, -97.206188*

School reunion was that evening. I lucked out. The Wayfarer Motel still had a couple of rooms left. Actually, it looked like it had been a long time since the Wayfarer had displayed its "No Vacancy" sign. As the saying goes, any port in a storm.

Sunday, May 27ᵗʰ - Hebron, NE, to Oak, NE - 26 miles

I left Hebron a little earlier than normal. After the previous day's slog, I was determined to finish this day before the worst of the heat set in. The wind had died down a bit overnight, but at sunrise was still blowing from the south at 15 mph. It was only supposed to get worse as the day progressed. I headed west nine miles to Deshler. Even with that crosswind it wasn't too bad. Then, turning north, I was pushed by a tailwind for the next five miles.

After crossing the Little Blue River I turned west again and started a stair-step route west and north along gravel roads towards the town of Oak. My plan was to make it to Edgar but the forecast was calling for severe thunderstorms with baseball-sized hail late in the afternoon and evening. I decided to split the ride to Edgar into two days. Hopefully that would give me a chance to get hunkered down in Oak before any nasty weather popped up.

For the next few days I rode along a section of the trail that followed the north side of the Little Blue River. Most of the historic sites I visited are associated with the Sioux, Cheyenne, and Arapaho uprising of August 7-9, 1864. At the time, emigrant traffic along the Oregon Trail was waning. The path along the Little Blue was mainly being used by freight wagons and stagecoaches going to and from Denver. Stations, called "road ranches," were built along the way to supply these travelers. Think of them as the 1860s version of a truck stop. Some were very elaborate, but many were little more than a lean-to.

By 1864, most of the Regular Army troops that were previously stationed on the frontier to keep the peace had been recalled to Civil War battlefields. The various tribes of the plains took this opportunity to first resume warfare with each other and, before long, against the white settlers. The 1864 uprising is unique because it represents one of the few times when different tribes successfully planned and executed a joint operation. The initial raids took place on August 7ᵗʰ. For weeks after that, travel on the Oregon Trail between Marysville, Kansas, and Julesburg, Colorado, came to a complete standstill. East of Fort

Kearny, Oak, Nebraska was the epicenter of the violence. The story may get a little confusing because I'm telling it in the order I came to the sites, not in the order the events actually occurred.

My first stop was at the site of Kiowa Station. This was one of the larger road ranches but nothing stands there now except a marker. As the trail upriver closed, westbound traffic bottled up at Kiowa Station. On August 9th, a stagecoach with seven impatient passengers started on the trail. About three miles west of the station the stagecoach began a slow climb up a ridge. The driver noticed Indians waiting in ambush within a draw near the river. He whirled the coach around and raced downhill back towards the station. The Indians set off in hot pursuit. Arrows and bullets flew in all directions, just like in the movies. As the stage made it to the safety of another oncoming wagon train, the Indians broke off their attack. The driver, Bob Emory, became a local hero.

A little further up the trail, I came to the site of the Bowie Ranch, where another attack took place. None of the details are known but the owner of the ranch and his wife were found dead beside the trail on August 9th. It's most likely they were killed and scalped by the same Indians that attacked Emory's stagecoach.

Still further up the trail, I passed the Oak Grove Ranch site. On August 7th, a group of local settlers had met at the ranch for a Sunday afternoon meal. A couple of Indians rode up and at first appeared friendly. Remember, these settlers were accustomed to friendly Indians moving through the area. They had lived in peace for years. Suddenly arrows were released and two white men dropped dead. The rest of the settlers ran inside a building and holed-up there until the Indians lost interest and went away. The next day, the survivors moved the dead men's bodies into the building and made a mad dash downriver to safety. The Indians returned and burned the station with the bodies inside. One of the escapees recalled seeing smoke rise behind them as they rode east. Today, a reconstructed ranch house and granite marker occupy the site.

Less than a quarter of a mile west of Oak Grove Station, several modern roads converge. A hundred yards or so beyond this intersection is where on August 7th, the first captive of the raids was taken. An old man and his two grandsons were riding a hay wagon back to their ranch, situated a few more miles upstream along the Little Blue. They were met at this spot by Indians, who killed and scalped the old man and his 13-year-old grandson immediately. The younger boy,

The cemetery at Oak, Nebraska, just prior to the annual Memorial Day ceremony. *40.232785, -97.873820*

The Narrows of the Little Blue River. The granite monument marks where, in 1929, Laura Roper said she was taken captive during the 1864 Indian raids. *40.252725, -97.929811*

seven-year-old Ambrose Asher, was carried away.

Up on a hilltop overlooking Oak Grove is the cemetery of the present day town of Oak. I rode up the hill to see if any of the names on the headstones were associated with the 1864 attacks. What happened next is one of the reasons people find bicycle touring so rewarding. It would have never happened to me if I was driving a car. I'll cherish this memory forever.

As I came to the cemetery, several people were placing flags on the graves of veterans. They were getting ready for Oak's annual Memorial Day ceremony. I was invited to stay for the occasion and to join them afterwards for a potluck lunch at the community center. Of course I accepted. As part of the ceremony, the local American Legion Post supplied an honor guard. The guard consisted of a flag bearer and a firing detail for a 21 gun salute. Unfortunately, they didn't have enough people to round out the detail properly. Being the good Air Force Reservist I was, and being well acquainted with the manual of arms, I asked if there was anything I could do to help. They smiled and handed me a Legion hat and an M-1 carbine. I really didn't want to be part of such a somber event dressed in a t-shirt and biker shorts so I went back to my bike and dug out my white long sleeved fishing shirt and my navy blue convertible pants. With the hat on, I almost matched their uniforms. At the appointed time, the flags were presented, three volleys fired, and Taps was played on a bugle. You cannot believe how honored I was to be a part of this.

After the ceremony at the cemetery, I cycled into Oak and joined the potluck festivities. When asked where I would be spending the night, I explained that I planned to camp in the town park up the road. They suggested I stay in the community center instead because of the threat of severe weather. Oak's community center is actually in the basement of the old school. It opened in the 1930s and closed in the 1970s. The basement is also the town's tornado shelter. I was warned to expect plenty of company if the weather turned bad.

Monday, May 28th - Oak, NE, to Edgar, NE - 15 miles

This turned out to be a really short day. I traveled only the remainder of the prior day's planned route. The nasty weather that had been predicted for the previous evening stayed well to the north. Oh well, better safe than sorry.

Two miles north of Oak, I linked up with a local rancher,

Ronda. I had spoken with her several months earlier by phone about visiting some historic sites now on the private property where she lives. She graciously agreed to give me the "royal tour" of the Eubank Ranch site and The Narrows of the Little Blue River.

In August 1864, William Eubank operated a road ranch about one half mile downstream of The Narrows. His father and nephew were the two people on the hay wagon that were killed on August 7th. Another nephew was Ambrose Asher, the seven-year-old boy who was captured. William lived with his wife Lucinda and four children at the ranch. About a mile upstream of The Narrows was another ranch, this one operated by Joe Roper. Joe's 16-year-old daughter, Laura, was a good friend of Lucinda Eubank. The Narrows, located between these two ranches, was a spot on the trail where the Little Blue River butted up so close to a steep bluff that wagons could barely squeeze through.

On August 7th, Laura Roper had gone to visit Lucinda at the Eubank ranch. Late in the afternoon, Laura started to walk home accompanied by Lucinda, William, and two of their children: Willie and Isabelle. As they approached The Narrows, William stopped to pull a sliver from his toe. All of a sudden, screaming was heard from back at the Eubank ranch. William ran towards the house but he was chased down and killed by Indians. At his house the other two Eubank children lay mortally wounded. Meanwhile at The Narrows, Laura, Lucinda, Willie, and Isabelle hid quietly in the bushes as the horror unfolded. When the Indians rode by, Isabelle cried out and all four were discovered.

The four captives were brought back to the Eubank ranch house. More Indians continued to arrive. With them was Ambrose Asher. After the house was ransacked, it was set ablaze. The Indians rode south to Kansas with Laura (age 16), Lucinda (age 23), Willie (age 6 months), Isabelle (age 3), and Ambrose (age 7).

Ronda and I went first to The Narrows. She was especially proud to show me an old tree next to the bluff that was there when the attacks took place. It's the only living witness to the tragedy. She then showed me a metal stake that had been driven into the ground by Laura Roper in 1929. Laura had returned to the site as part of a 65th anniversary of the event. She drove the stake at the spot where she remembered being captured. The current landowner set the stake into concrete and placed a stone marker, at his own expense, to commemorate the site.

Ronda then took me to where the actual Eubank ranch once

stood. In 1864, the ranch was situated on the banks of the river. In the intervening years, however, the course of the river has shifted west. While walking near the site we flushed a wild turkey hen from her nest. I counted ten eggs. I'm sure the bird returned as soon as we left. Back at Ronda's ranch, she told me I was the first bicyclist to ever visit the sites. She had taken busloads of school kids, wagon train re-enactors, and even motorcyclists to the landmarks, but never a bicyclist.

After thanking Ronda for taking the time to give me a tour, I continued on my short ride to Edgar. I passed several old farm houses that looked abandoned. At one such place a dog came out to meet me. He wasn't aggressive. He just looked like he wanted some company. I tried several times to get him to go back to the house but he kept following me. Occasionally he'd run off into a field but within a minute or two he was back at my side again. I hoped he would find his way home. After traveling together for about five miles, we came into Edgar. All of a sudden it looked like he remembered where he was. He took off running and that's the last I saw of him. I suspect someone in town had taken Fido out to the country and abandoned him. Now, it seemed, he was back on familiar turf.

As I rode downtown, I found only one store open. Everything else was closed for Memorial Day. I went into the grocery store and asked about camping. The owner made a few calls and I was told I could camp in the city park on the south side of town. Restrooms were available at the nearby cemetery. I don't know if it was a hint but I was also told the city swimming pool was open and I was welcomed to use the showers. I did. Showers, especially free ones, are a luxury seldom passed up by bicycle tourists. Baby wipes are the usual fallback option.

When I arrived at the park I was met by Harold and Linda. They were camping there in their RV. Before I could even unpack my gear, they invited me to join them and some other friends for lunch. We spent the rest of the afternoon visiting.

Tuesday, May 29th - Edgar, NE, to Hastings, NE - 52 miles

Finally the wind started to be more favorable. I headed west from Edgar and made the 11 miles to Deweese in no time. I knew Deweese had one restaurant but I wasn't sure if it was open for breakfast. It wasn't. As I rode by the post office, the postmaster called out to me. I turned around and went back to talk. He said he saw the bike and wanted to know where I was going. I think he just wanted a new face to talk to. After I filled him in about my journey, he and a customer gave me the low-down on Deweese. The town, like so many rural towns in the area, was dying. In the 1990s, the rail line that served the town was taken out of service. The grain elevator closed. Without jobs, the young people had no choice but to move away. The aging population was dwindling. He said there were only about 60 residents left.

It was another stair-step ride north and west. Some of the roads were paved, others not. I was still following the north side of the Little Blue River. All along the way, I passed markers at the sites of various road ranches. Each of these ranches has a story, but the most important one, as far as the 1864 raids were concerned, was Pawnee Ranch. This ranch was the most fortified of all the ranches in the area. It was also the most easily defended. Pawnee Ranch was located at the confluence of Pawnee Creek and the Little Blue River. As word of the violence spread up and down the trail, families started gathering their possessions and moving to Pawnee Ranch for protection. Ultimately, over 70 people sought refuge and waited for the inevitable. The feared attack finally came on the afternoon of August 10th. For hours, the Indians tried all their favorite tricks to breach the defenses. None worked. They eventually gave up and went away. On the following day all the defenders left the ranch together. Soon after, the ranch was burned.

Next I rode towards Indian Hollow. This small draw, located 3.7 miles northeast of Ayr, drains south towards the Little Blue. On the morning of August 7th, a train consisting of six freight wagons was rolling down into the draw. In what was probably the first of the attacks along the Little Blue River, the train was hit with a shower of arrows. Five of the six drivers were immediately dropped. The sixth driver, with one arrow stuck in his forehead and another in his torso, somehow managed to escape into a field of tall sunflowers. The Indians didn't find him. The next day, travelers from nearby Thirty-Two Mile Station came upon the wrecked wagons, the five dead drivers, and the lone survivor. His body was black and swollen from exposure and contorted with pain but miraculously he had made it through the night. He lived just long enough to tell his story. All six victims were buried in a common grave above the hollow.

As I approached this ambush site, I had to detour around an open trench across the road. The road was closed to cars but the workers allowed me to walk my bike around the construction area

Marker placed by the Boy Scouts in 1931 to commemorate the mass grave of eight (probably only six) teamsters killed in Indian Hollow on August 7, 1864. *40.480143, -98.392182*

and get to the interpretive marker. In another one of my moments of pure chance, the landowner arrived to check on the progress of the work. I told him, Brian, of my trip and my interest in the attacks along the Little Blue River. He asked if I wanted to visit the burial site. Of course I did! He pointed to two small stakes on a ridge just south of the marker. I walked up to the crest, about a hundred yards away. There I saw a plaque that had been placed on the grave by Boy Scouts back in 1931. The plaque said eight men were buried here, but all the accounts I've read refer to only six. Maybe two victims from another attack were buried here also, but I doubt it. The Boy Scouts were probably wrong.

I continued following the trail past two more stations and soon arrived at Prairie Lakes Recreation Area. This was my planned camping spot for the night. But when I saw the park I had second thoughts. It was pitiful. Broken glass was everywhere. That's something bicyclists avoid like the plague. Graffiti covered the walls of what could only loosely be called a bathroom. Nebraska should be ashamed of that park. Even we in Louisiana know it's better to close a park than to simply abandon it. Not another soul was within sight. I had no intention of becoming just another unmarked grave on the Oregon Trail. I moved on.

After backtracking five miles to Hastings, I grabbed a room at the first motel I came to, the X-L Motel. It was old but clean and it was in much better shape than the Wayfarer Motel back in Hebron. Like many of the motels built in the late 1950s, the eaves around the roof were trimmed with orange and green neon lights. Very nostalgic.

Wednesday, May 30th - Hunkered Down in Hastings, NE - 0 miles

I woke up early, hoping to be on the road again by 6:00 a.m. When I checked the weather radar, though, I saw there were thunderstorms already building up west of Kearney. I really didn't want to sit around another day so I loaded up the bike and stepped outside. To the west, lightning was already flashing on the horizon. I saw no use in being stupid, so I walked over to the motel lobby and paid for another night. At the convenience store next door, I stocked up on all the necessities of motel camping: Dr. Pepper, chips, pre-packaged sandwiches, and one (yes, only one) chocolate bar. I was now set for the apocalypse. A few hours later the storms hit Hastings. High winds, heavy rain, lightning, and even some hail came in waves throughout the day. It would have been dangerous to be on a bicycle in this weather so I settled in to a day of channel surfing. I probably needed a rest day anyway.

Thursday, May 31st - Hastings, NE, to Kearney, NE - 47 miles

After two nights at the X-L Motel I was eager to get on the road again. A few days earlier I was dealing with record heat. Now it was downright cold. I was glad I had a pair of merino wool long johns with me. Once I was sufficiently bundled up I rolled out the door and headed west. My thin gloves weren't much help. By the time I reached Kennesaw, my hands were blue and numb. Like Deweese, Kennesaw appeared to be gasping for its final breath. An official looking sign along the road offered free lots in town to anyone willing to move there and build a house. Honestly, it didn't seem like a bad place to retire to so long as a job wasn't needed. I stopped at the local convenience store and got an egg sandwich and some juice. I sat inside just long enough to thaw out a bit before riding on.

A few miles north of Kennesaw, I arrived at the grave of Susan Haile. As in the case of George Winslow, Susan is famous mainly

Susan Haile pioneer grave, just south of Denman, Nebraska. *40.655325, -98.713367*

Reconstructed Pawnee earthen lodge at the Great River Road Archway Museum in Kearney, Nebraska. *40.671792, -99.039605*

because we actually know something about her. She was born in Cape Girardeau, Missouri, in 1817. In 1836 she married, and by 1852 she had six kids. Susan, her husband Richard, and their children left Missouri in the spring of 1852. Traveling with her immediate family were her unmarried sister and her brother's family. Along the Oregon Trail in 1852, cholera was especially rampant. On June 2nd, within sight of the Platte River, Susan died. Legends abound of loved ones returning to trail gravesites years later, usually pushing a wheelbarrow, to place elaborate headstones. Although there is no family record of this in Susan's case, something similar must have happened. Two years later, in 1854, another passing emigrant wrote in his diary that Susan's grave was marked by a fine marble headstone. On this day, the loneliness of her grave was made even more striking to me by the gray skies and the cold wind blowing across the prairie. The grave is on a small knoll, and nearby wagon swales are still plainly visible. Next to her headstone were many small trinkets. I suspected these were geocaching items but to me they just trivialized the site. My visit to her grave took place two days shy of the 160th anniversary of her death. I wondered if it was such a cold and windy day when she passed on.

From Susan Haile's grave I rode almost straight west to Fort Kearny (note that the spelling is different from the town of Kearney). Fort Kearny opened for business in 1848, just in time for the gold rush that began the following spring. It was strategically located at the point where all the branches of the Oregon Trail came together. Like most of the plains forts of the era, Fort Kearny didn't originally have walls. It was just a collection of buildings arranged around a parade field. Its main goals were to keep the peace along the trail and to provide assistance to the travelers as needed. Many pioneers wrote of the irony that all the fort's cannons were pointed at their own buildings and fired only during ceremonies. After the 1864 Indian raids, however, four separate palisades were built. These enclosures weren't for the troops' protection, though. Their purpose was to keep the cattle and horses from being stampeded by the Indians. Following the completion of the Transcontinental Railroad in 1869, wagon travel declined. The fort was deactivated in 1871.

While at Fort Kearny, I was escorted by Bill Peterson. He's the current president of the Nebraska Chapter of the Oregon-California Trails Association. As we walked around the grounds Bill shared many behind-the-scenes stories about the fort. It's dedicated people like him that keep the trail alive for the rest of us. Unlike the Frontier Trails

Museum in Independence, the Fort Kearny museum is up-to-date. It was well worth the time I spent there.

When I finished my visit at the fort, I biked the last seven miles into the town of Kearney. For 2012, the cycling part of my journey had ended.

Friday, June 1st - Around Kearney, NE - 0 miles

The morning started off cold and drizzly. It was the perfect day to be inside a museum. Thankfully, Kearney has just such a place: The Great Platte River Road Archway. It's actually built into an arch that spans over Interstate 80. It's the place Jack Nicholson visited near the end of the film, *About Schmidt*. The museum highlights the role of the Platte River valley as a corridor to the west. Displays begin with the emigrant trails, followed by the railroads, the Lincoln Highway, and modern Interstate 80. Outside the main building several living history exhibits have also been created. Since the weather was dreary, I was the only one foolish enough to visit these displays. I had plenty of time to talk with the re-enactors.

One of the exhibits was a reconstructed Pawnee earthen lodge. Michael, the host, was a Pawnee himself. A student at Fort Lewis College in Durango, Colorado, he was doing a summer internship at the museum. We talked at length about Pawnee history and culture. According to Michael, the Pawnee originally lived in villages throughout Nebraska and Kansas. Each village usually contained about ten lodges similar to the one on display. The Pawnee were not as nomadic as other plains tribes, but they did go on two major buffalo hunts each year. As eastern tribes were forced west, the Pawnee were squeezed into smaller and smaller areas. Eventually they were forced onto reservations in Oklahoma.

Another outside exhibit was a pioneer sod house. Without a good supply of building materials, many little houses on the prairie were constructed from blocks of sod cut from the land itself. My host here was Megan. She was originally from Fairbury. She studied music but her love of history landed her a permanent job at the museum. She explained to me that sod homes ranged from the very simple to the very elaborate depending on the engineering abilities of the builder. Some pioneers brought with them a wealth of knowledge about construction. Megan also pointed out the garden next to the house. It was planted with only the crops that would have been used during the 1800s. Some of the plants I recognized but many were unfamiliar to me. She said it took about one quarter acre of land to sustain one person for one year.

The second half of the day was spent taking care of the logistics of getting my gear home. I took all my camping equipment, my tools, my extra clothes, and my panniers to the local UPS store. They boxed everything up for me, weighed it, and readied it for shipment. As usual, I didn't want the hassle of carrying anything with me through the airport. Then I rode my bike over to the Bike Shed, one of only two bike shops in Kearney. They boxed up the bike and trailer and sent it home to Louisiana.

The Fate of the Captives

Some pages back, I told you about five people taken captive by the Indians during the raids of 1864 near Oak, Nebraska. So as not to leave you wondering, here's what became of them. The five Oak captives were quickly spirited south into Kansas. There they were joined by two additional captives taken from a wagon train which was attacked near Plum Creek, Nebraska. The two new prisoners were Nancy Morton (age 19) and Danny Marble (age 9). Nancy's husband and Danny's father were among those killed in the attack (more about them in the next chapter). All seven captives were led by the Cheyenne into western Kansas and then into Colorado. In September the Cheyenne traded Nancy Morton, Lucinda Eubank, and Willie Eubank to the Sioux. Through miscommunication, the Cheyenne thought Isabelle Eubank was Laura Roper's daughter, so Lucinda and Isabelle became separated.

On September 18, 1864, the Cheyenne released Laura Roper, Isabelle Eubank, Ambrose Asher, and Danny Marble to the Army in Denver. Isabelle had suffered too much in captivity and died soon after the release. At the time, Danny appeared healthy and was taken in by the soldiers while waiting to be sent back east to his mother. Before the arrangements could be finalized, however, Danny contracted typhoid fever and died at the Army hospital. Ambrose did make it back to his parents, and he lived until 1894. He died in the town of California, Missouri.

Laura Roper also survived. In 1929, if you recall, she returned to The Narrows and drove a stake into the ground at her place of capture. I've seen a photograph of her next to the stake, and in the background is the same old oak tree I saw when I visited The Narrows. Laura died in 1930 in Enid, Oklahoma.

The three remaining prisoners were taken by the Sioux further north into Wyoming. Nancy Morton was then traded to the Shoshone and carried off into Montana and possibly Idaho. A trapper bargained for her and in February, 1865, brought her into Fort Laramie, Wyoming. Nancy died in 1912 in Jefferson, Iowa.

Lucinda and Willie Eubank were held the longest. They were eventually turned over by the Sioux to the Army at Fort Laramie in May, 1865. For the rest of her life, Lucinda refused to believe her daughter Isabelle had died. Lucinda passed away in 1913 in McCune, Kansas. Her son Willie outlived all the other captives. He lived until 1935 and died in Pierce, Colorado.

So there you have it, the rest of the story. The more you study history, the more you come to realize that these events, the Indian Wars and the settling of the west, were not that long ago. My parents were both born before the last of the Oak captives had passed away.

Up Along the Plattes 2013

My second year along the Oregon Trail began where it ended in 2012, in Kearney, Nebraska. Mostly I followed the Platte River or one of its two main tributaries: the South Platte and the North Platte. The South Platte River begins in Colorado and flows northeast into Nebraska. The headwaters of the North Platte River also originate in Colorado, but its course makes a wide swing northward into Wyoming before flowing southeast into Nebraska. Both come together near the present-day city of North Platte, Nebraska. The wide valleys formed by these rivers provided the pioneers with a perfect corridor to approach the Rocky Mountains. The route became known as the Great Platte River Road, and upon it passed the Oregon Trail, the California Trail, the Mormon Trail, and the Pony Express Trail. Telegraph lines were built through the corridor. Rail lines followed. The Lincoln Highway, U.S. Highway 30, and eventually Interstate 80 all stayed within sight of one of the Plattes. So did I, all the way to Casper, Wyoming.

Near Kearney, the surrounding land was still dominated by farms. Amber waves of grain slowly gave way to open range. The short grass prairie beside the North Platte River soon became dotted with the sandstone monoliths recorded by the emigrants in their journals: Court House Rock, Chimney Rock, and Scott's Bluff. Cattle grazed where the buffalo once roamed. I didn't see many deer, but the antelope still played.

As I rode west I was also climbing. You don't notice it much in a car going 75 miles per hour, but on a bike every foot of elevation gain is felt. Kearney sits at 2,154 feet above sea level. By the time I reached Casper, I was 3,000 feet higher. The elevation of my front yard is 7 feet above the Gulf of Mexico. My legs and my lungs could feel the difference.

I also felt the dryness. By Louisiana standards, the Platte River valley is a desert. But as I headed higher and further west, the humidity

Pioneer log cabin and schoolhouse, relocated to the Trails and Rails Museum, Kearney, Nebraska. *40.684244, -99.092409*

The Platte River, appearing much the same as during the Oregon Trail days. *40.683429, -99.636782*

dropped even more. I drank increasing amounts of water but within a few days my lips were severely chapped. Even with the benefits of sunscreen and lip balm I often woke in the mornings with my lips painfully glued together. Though the pioneers didn't write much about it, they too must have had similar experiences. Bleeding lips and salt crusted skin were never a part of the Westerns I saw on TV.

Monday, June 3ʳᵈ - Back in Kearney, NE

When I arrived in Kearney, it was hard for me to believe a year had already passed. My bike and gear were waiting for me as expected at the hotel, courtesy of FedEx. Once I was rested from the flight, I started putting things together. This had become second nature by now. The one big change from the previous year was a new bike. Actually, it was mostly the same bike but with a new frame and fork. In 2012, my ride was done on an old aluminum framed hardtail mountain bike. I replaced it with a steel touring bike frame. Touring bikes have a longer wheel base so the steering isn't as twitchy. Also, steel absorbs those bumps in the road much better than aluminum. Other than the frame and fork, though, most of the remaining parts were the same. I just transferred them from one frame to the other.

I spent the day riding around Kearney and seeing the town. It was cold and rainy when I was there in 2012. Now it was warm and sunny, perfect for sightseeing. The first order of business was to find a grocery store and stock up on all the essentials of a bicycle touring menu. Basically that included the triad of breakfast bars, peanut butter, and tortillas. Next, I visited a bike shop to get a bottle of chain lube. I forgot to pack some in my box for shipment and I knew the airport TSA folks would consider it a deadly weapon if I tried to smuggle it on the plane with me.

After finishing my errands, I visited the Trails and Rails Museum. It's run by the Buffalo County Historical Society and is located directly on the Mormon Trail. An old steam engine, a flatcar, and a caboose are among their collection of railroad items. A number of old buildings have also been brought to the museum. These include cabins, churches, and schoolhouses. I was given a personal tour of the museum grounds by Wyatt. His summer job was tour guide but during the rest of the year he was a physics student at the University of Nebraska - Kearney.

The Mormon Trail is another National Historic Trail. In pioneer days, nobody thought of it as a distinct trail until it branched off from the Oregon Trail at Fort Bridger, Wyoming. Trails existed on both sides along the Platte River. Some modern authors claim the Mormons stayed on the north side of the river and the Oregon and California bound travelers stayed on the south side. Contemporary writers of the period, however, said both sides were used almost equally by everyone. What mattered most was where the wagon trains were starting from. If they began on the north side of the Platte River at Council Bluffs, Iowa, or Winter Quarters, Nebraska, they tended to stay on the north side. But if the wagons started west from Independence, St. Joseph, or Nebraska City, they favored the south side. Crossing the Platte River from one bank to the other was not a simple task.

Leaving the museum, I continued to ride around Kearney. Even with a population of only 32,000 people, the town has found the will and the resources to build over 20 miles of paved bicycle and pedestrian pathways. In Baton Rouge, we have ten times the population and only half the mileage of paved trails. It all comes down to priorities.

Later that evening I had dinner with Bill Peterson. I met him in 2012 at Fort Kearny and, if you recall, he was the president of the Nebraska Chapter of OCTA. We reviewed my maps and he gave me some suggestions for lesser known sites to visit along the way.

Tuesday, June 4th – Kearney, NE, to Lexington, NE – 46 miles

Bad weather struck Kearney overnight but was well to the east by sunrise. After eating the free breakfast at the hotel, I was on the road by 7:30 a.m. I crossed to the south side of the Platte River and soon turned westward along the Oregon Trail. For the next 22 miles I rode on one of the straightest and flattest roads I've ever seen. If it wasn't for the brisk crosswind from the north it would have been ideal.

With a couple of jogs to the north and west, I finally came to the site of the Plum Creek Massacre. I wrote earlier about the 1864 Indian uprising in the area. On August 8th, the day after the killings along the Little Blue River, three separate wagon trains were attacked along Plum Creek, about 11 miles southeast of Lexington, Nebraska. They weren't intentionally traveling together but they shared a common campground the night before. On the morning of the attack, the three groups broke camp at about the same time. After a few miles on the trail, Indians were seen approaching from the high ground to the south. Some of the wagons turned north towards the river and others turned south towards the hills. None made it to safety. All thirteen men were killed. Eleven were later buried next to the road in a common grave. The other two men were buried near the river, but their graves have long since washed away. The common grave is still unmarked but historians are well aware of its location. Only three people survived the attack. One woman, Mrs. James Smith, hid in the tall reeds by the river and escaped detection. She was later rescued by soldiers, but soon went insane. Nancy Morton (age 19) and Danny Marble (age 9) were captured. Their fates were revealed in the previous chapter.

A little more about Nancy Morton to flesh out the story: Nancy was born in 1845. At the age of 15 she married Frank Morton. By the summer of 1863 the couple had two children. Measles struck the family and both children died. A year later, in 1864, it was suggested to Nancy that a trip to Denver with her husband, her brother, and a cousin might be just the thing to help her move on. By her own accounts the trip had been a pleasant one up until that fateful morning when she and Danny Marble were taken prisoner. In 1891, Nancy recounted in her memoir that, as she was being carried off south by the Indians, she had a miscarriage.

A mile and a half west of the massacre site is the Plum Creek Cemetery. For years it was known as the Plum Creek Massacre Cemetery. Finally someone realized that none of the massacre victims were actually buried there so they changed the name. In fact, there is only one confirmed grave in the cemetery. In 1963, the grave of an unidentified emigrant child was exposed by erosion a few miles away. A new coffin was obtained and the child was re-interred in the cemetery. The location of the cemetery is close to some historic road ranches and a small cavalry outpost so it's very likely other graves are nearby. None, however, have been positively located. Another headstone in the cemetery is for Sarepta Fly. The whereabouts of her grave have been lost but long ago children found her headstone in a farmer's field. In 1930, it was moved to the cemetery for preservation. Sarepta was 24 years old when she died in 1865.

After leaving the cemetery, I continued to ride along dirt roads on the south side of the Platte until I reached the Robb Ranch. There I met Joe, the owner of the ranch. He was a retired veterinarian and rancher and the land had been in his family since 1874. He had a wealth of knowledge not only about Oregon Trail history but Nebraska history in general. The Oregon Trail passed right through his ranch. Plum Creek still does. The upper crossing of Plum Creek was just south of his house and he showed me where the pioneers had dug ramps along the banks of the creek to make the crossing easier. The cut-outs were still visible. As we walked near the creek, he said it was safe to walk through the marijuana but stay clear of the thistles. Most people don't realize marijuana grows wild in Kansas and Nebraska. Of course, the natural variety has no potency and hence no value. According to Joe, however, it will tear up a lawnmower.

Joe then showed me his vast collection of bicycles. The one that caught my eye was an "ordinary" bike. The head badge said "Boneshaker – Cincinnati, Ohio." Originally, bicycles had a large wheel in front and a small wheel in back. They were sometimes called Penny-Farthings and had a reputation for causing lots of pain. A later design, similar in most respects to today's bicycles, was referred to as a "safety bike." The older style then became known as an "ordinary." Joe asked me if I wanted to give the ordinary bike a try. At first I said no, but as I thought about it I knew I would regret not riding one when I had the chance. Joe, at age 76, rode it first to prove he still could. To make it easier for me, I mounted the bike from the fender of a trailer parked next to Joe's driveway. It didn't help much. After ten feet or so I went over the handlebars. Once was enough. There was no use being stubborn about it.

I said goodbye to Joe and rode ten more miles north to Lexington. In town I paid a visit to the Dawson County History Museum where I was able to look at a photocopy of Nancy Morton's original account of her capture. It was strange to be able to read her story in her own handwriting. Next to the museum was a city park where I camped for the night.

Wednesday, June 5th – Lexington, NE, to Brady, NE – 62 miles

I've slept in much better places than the Lexington city park. I pitched my tent under the pavilion for some added shelter, so that wasn't bad. The restrooms at the pavilion were supposed to be left unlocked for me. They weren't. Luckily there was a porta-potty within walking distance. The real fun began around 10:00 p.m. I heard a car circling through the park very slowly. I peeked out the window of my tent and saw what looked like a low-rider Celica making the rounds. I didn't think too much about it the first time but he came back again. And again. I wasn't sure what he was looking for but obviously he was up to no good. I finally called the police and within minutes a patrol car arrived. I talked with the officer for a while and he promised to swing by the park from time to time. I never saw the other car again. The icing on the cake, however, was when all the lights of the pavilion came on automatically at midnight. I guess the town was trying to keep people from stealing picnic tables after dark.

When morning finally arrived, I didn't waste much time packing and getting on the road. It wasn't that Lexington was a bad place but for me it just wasn't very restful. I crossed to the south side of the Platte again and started a zig-zag to the northwest. Even though the "official" route of the Oregon Trail is on the south side of the river, all of the eventual development occurred on the other side. The railroad, the stage lines, the modern highways, and all of the towns were, and still are, on the north side. Also, the trail generally heads northwest but the roads in Nebraska are built along one mile section lines. This meant riding north a mile or two, then west a mile or two, then repeating it over and over. Historians even refer to this stretch of the trail as the "Gothenburg Stair-Step."

Imagine taking a spinning class at the local gym and staying on the bike for eight hours. That pretty much sums up the day's ride. I started off from Lexington in a light rain. Nothing heavy, just enough to have to put on the rain gear. It only lasted for an hour. When it stopped the wind picked up, and naturally it had to be from the northwest. The rest of the day I battled 15-20 mph headwinds or crosswinds. For 62 miles my average speed was only 7.7 mph. It's not the farthest I've ridden in one day, but it seemed like the longest.

There was only one landmark I wanted to visit on this leg of the trail. In the town of Gothenberg there is a well-known Pony Express station. But south of town there is another station that's seldom visited. That is the one I wanted to see. When I got to the road leading to it, though, the gravel was so loose and the headwind was so strong I could barely keep my front wheel straight. Then I heard a voice say, "This is NOT the road you're looking for." Now who am I to question the Force? I turned my bike around and headed back to the pavement.

As it turned out, about the only exciting thing I saw during the morning was a group of several hundred cyclists all heading in the opposite direction. Of course, they had the tailwind. The riders were part of the 2013 Bike Ride Across Nebraska (BRAN).

Most of the day was spent riding along what Nebraskan's call their "South Coast." Eventually I turned north towards the town of

Brady. Brady is a very small farming community. I arrived in town late in the afternoon and went to their park. It's mainly baseball fields, but along one side is a small picnic area. I had permission to camp there overnight. After setting up the tent, I was able to watch a Little League game before turning in for the evening. It was much more relaxing than the night before.

Thursday, June 6ᵗʰ - Brady, NE, to Sutherland, NE - 52 miles

It's amazing how much the weather can change in ten hours. When I went to sleep the wind was still howling, but by morning it was perfectly calm. The temperature was so cool I could actually see my breath.

After leaving Brady, my first stop of the day was at the statue of a soldier where the flagpole of Fort McPherson once stood. Fort McPherson, originally called Camp Cottonwood, was built in 1866 to protect trail travelers and settlers in the area. It was located near the mouth of Cottonwood Creek, a favorite route for Indian migrations. The fort was deactivated in 1880. As Fort McPherson was being taken out of service, the post's cemetery was designated a National Cemetery. Throughout the 1880s, as other frontier forts were also being closed, the remains from their cemeteries were relocated to Fort McPherson. There was one marker I particularly wanted to visit. The enlisted soldiers that died in the Grattan Battle of 1854, in Wyoming, were reburied in a common grave at Fort McPherson. Their fearless leader, since he was an officer, was shipped back to Fort Leavenworth, Kansas, for a more personalized interment.

From Fort McPherson I biked west to Sioux Lookout. Sioux Lookout is the highest point in North Platte County. Supposedly the Sioux and other tribes would use the spot to keep an eye on wagons and troops moving in the valley below. In the 1930s, a granite statue of a Sioux warrior was dragged up to the summit by a horse and rider and set into place. After being on guard for almost 70 years, it was finally hauled back down. Generations of sharpshooters had reduced the mighty warrior to a rock pillar. The statue was restored and now stands on the North Platte courthouse lawn. Sioux Lookout is on private, fenced, property. At one time an interpretive marker was located along the road but even that was now missing.

I stopped for lunch in the city of North Platte and then rode on. About ten miles west of town, traces of the original trail can be

Statue of an Indian Wars era soldier placed where the flag pole of Fort McPherson once stood. *41.016483, -100.517837*

Looking down from Windlass Hill into Ash Hollow. Ash Hollow State Historical Park, Nebraska. *41.261777, -102.115733*

seen. As they cut across the prairie, the swales created by the wagons cause rainwater to puddle on the surface of the ground. This, in turn, causes the grass to be a little thicker and greener wherever the wagons roamed.

As I headed to Sutherland Reservoir, my planned campsite for the night, I passed just south of O'Fallons Bluff. When the wagon trains reached this point, they could no longer follow near the south edge of the river. They had to climb the bluff. A rest area on the eastbound side of Interstate 80 has a short walking path to marked swales. This area, however, is inaccessible to westbound drivers on the highway and cyclists on county roads. I had to skip it. I arrived at Sutherland Reservoir early enough to wander around the campground for a while. The campground was primitive. There was no water or electricity but it was very well maintained. On the opposite side of a canal I saw the buildings of the park's maintenance yard. I crossed a bridge to get to the property but the gate was locked. Since there wasn't any water in the campground, and since my water bottles were almost empty, I decided to climb over the gate. Once inside the yard, I found a water spigot and topped off my bottles. No harm done. I was in and out in no time. Back at my campsite, I settled in for a peaceful evening. I was the only camper there.

Friday, June 7th - Sutherland, NE, to Brule, NE - 51 miles

I made another early start since the forecast was calling for more severe weather in the afternoon. This, unfortunately, is as common on the plains today as it was 170 years ago. I don't know if the forecasting is any better but at least with modern weather radar the really bad stuff can't sneak up on you. I didn't get rained on during the day, but the heat and wind were brutal.

When I passed by the city of North Platte on the previous day, I left behind the wide flat valley of the Platte River. Just east of North Platte (the city), the Platte River splits into the North Platte River and the South Platte River. Emigrants traveling on the south side of the Platte continued westward along the south side of the South Platte River until the river could be forded. The first suitable place was at California Crossing. It was located about four miles west of present-day Brule. After the rivers divide, the hills on the south side move closer to the water. The pioneers were able to stay next to the river but now that space is occupied by Interstate 80. This forced me to take parallel county roads one mile south of the Interstate. These roads were in the hills, and probably 40 of the 50 miles I rode were on gravel. In a couple of places, the gravel was so deep I not only had to push the bike uphill, but also downhill. There just wasn't any traction. I kept remembering the advice Dr. Marcus Whitman gave to the members of the Great Migration: "Keep moving, for nothing else will bring you to your goal." So keep moving I did.

As I turned north and crossed the Interstate and the South Platte River near Brule, I stopped at a convenience store for some Gatorade. While soaking up the air conditioning, I overheard another customer ask about the campground next door. Even though I had already made plans to camp in Brule's town park, I wondered if this campground had showers. I asked, and they did. They charged me $7.00 to take a shower, but it was well worth the money to shed four days of sweat, sunscreen, and Nebraska dust.

A mile or so further brought me to the park. I had spoken with BJ, Brule's community events chairperson, a few months earlier. She was my contact for getting permission to camp in town. Shortly before this year's ride, BJ e-mailed me again to verify the date. She wanted to schedule the town's annual potluck dinner to coincide with my visit. The pavilion at the park was empty when I got there. I took a quick nap until BJ showed up. Before long, other folks started to arrive, each bringing a dish of food for the evening. I didn't count, but I think about 50 people attended. Before the evening was over, I had several invitations to spend the night at different homes. BJ asked first, so instead of camping, I slept comfortably in BJ and her husband John's guestroom.

Saturday, June 8th - Brule, NE, to Lewellen, NE - 38 miles

With the change from Central Time to Mountain Time, I was on the road by 6:00 a.m. Four miles out of Brule I came to my first landmark of the day, California Hill. After the pioneers crossed the South Platte, they had to make their way up California Hill to get on the plateau that separates the two rivers. It was a difficult climb. People were often forced to offload part of their cargo to lighten the wagons. Deep ruts can still be seen on the side of the hill. It took the 1843 Great Migration five days to ford the river. While waiting, the first recorded birth of a white child on the Oregon Trail occurred. It was also near this crossing that Dr. Marcus Whitman met up with the Great Migration.

In 1836 Marcus Whitman and his wife Narcissa had traveled west with two other missionaries and a group of fur traders. As I've stated before, the Whitmans established a mission near Walla Walla, Washington. In 1842, Dr. Whitman received word that support for the mission was coming to an end. He rushed back east and successfully pleaded his case. On the return trip west he was delayed in St. Louis but then traveled quickly to catch up with the wagon train. I don't know if he attended the birth of the child but from here on he became the train's unofficial guide. Few men other than Dr. Whitman had already crossed the continent twice on the Oregon Trail. This would be his third trip.

By the time I arrived at the base of California Hill, raindrops were beginning to fall. The dirt road leading up was already muddy, so I parked my bike and walked to the summit. From there I was able to look back down into the South Platte River valley. Through the heavy mist I could barely make out the river below. I tried to imagine what an effort it must have been to get a 2,000 pound wagon up a muddy slope. Walking up was hard enough.

Back on the bike, I continued west from California Hill for another five miles. Then I turned north and began my own crossing of the plateau. I rode straight into a cold north wind. Before long, I started seeing lightning to my left. As I passed each farm house I calculated whether or not I could get to the next house without being struck first. Against the wind and the rain it took me over two hours to ride the ten miles to my next turn. At U.S. Highway 26 I turned west again and soon arrived at Windlass Hill, the emigrant's entry point into Ash Hollow. It's a very steep descent. Legend has it that wagons were occasionally lowered into the valley with the aid of a windlass (a rope wrapped around a shaft attached to a crank, like you see above an old water well), but there is no documented evidence of this. What the pioneers did do, however, was lock their wagon wheels with heavy chains and let them skid down the hill. If they weren't careful the wagons could run over the oxen in front of them. Thousands of wagons skidding down Windlass Hill created deep ruts. Years of erosion has since made these ruts all the more dramatic. A reconstructed sod house sits at the bottom of Windlass Hill. As I was looking at it, the light rain turned into a downpour. I dashed inside and waited for about 15 minutes until the squall passed. The roof on this house didn't leak, but supposedly the original ones leaked like a sieve.

At Ash Hollow, in 1841, the first recorded death by accidental gunfire happened on the trail. In an almost perfect case of historical irony, a member of the Bidwell-Bartleson party by the name of James Shotwell was killed when he tried to remove a shotgun, barrel first, from his wagon. It was loaded. The hammer snagged on something and then broke free, sending it forward to strike the primer. He probably took the full load in his chest.

The cemetery at Ash Hollow also contains one of the best known trailside graves. Rachel Pattison was an 18-year-old newlywed. She was married on April 3, 1849, and a week later headed west from Illinois with her husband Nathan and members of his immediate family. Her group arrived at Ash Hollow on June 18th, and by the following morning Rachel was ill with cholera. She died that evening. Nathan continued on to Oregon but never remarried.

Just past Ash Hollow, I left the highway and turned down a long dirt road to the Signal Bluff Ranch. It is a working farm and ranch owned by John and Nancy. Both are Oregon Trail enthusiasts. In addition to the ranch, they have a guesthouse next to their home called Nancy B's Backyard Bunkhouse. That's where I stopped for the night.

Sunday, June 9ᵗʰ - Lewellen, NE, to Bridgeport, NE - 56 miles

My original plan was to ride across Signal Ranch in the morning and connect with another county road about two miles northwest. When John and I scoped out the route the previous afternoon, though, he convinced me it wasn't safe to cross. Tall grass completely covered the trail. The area, according to John, was heavily infested with rattlesnakes. I had no reason to believe otherwise. If I were a rattlesnake, that's where I'd hang out. Without being able to see the ground, it would have been foolish to ride a bike or walk through the grass without snake boots.

So the day started with John hauling me and my gear over his property to his neighbor's farm two miles away. I was glad he offered to do this. It would have taken me forever to walk my bike across the field watching for rattlesnakes with each step. Along the way, we passed Signal Bluff, the inspiration for the name of John and Nancy's ranch. John said there was a trail up to the top and tepee rings could still be seen among the rocks. Signal Bluff extends to the North Platte River closer than any other outcropping, so it was a prime lookout point for the Indians. John also showed me a clump of trees where an old sod house once stood. Some years ago, a 92 year-old-man visited

John and claimed he grew up in that house. John warned him about the snakes in the grass. The old man laughed and said they were just as bad when he lived there. He recalled finding them in the house all the time.

When we got to his neighbor's farm, I offloaded my stuff from John's truck and thanked him for his hospitality. The owner of the farm wasn't stirring yet, but one of his dogs was awake and very curious. He watched closely as I put everything back on the bike. Then he started following me. Like the stray dog back in Edgar, Kansas, this dog just wouldn't turn around. For six miles he tracked me all the way to the intersection at Highway 27 near Oshkosh. Near that junction is a golf course so I stopped to see if someone would hold onto the dog until I was further down the road. A man in the parking lot recognized him and knew its owner. He made a phone call and said the guy would come and get him. With the problem solved, I rode on.

Just north of the golf course along the highway is another pioneer grave. This one belongs to John Hollman. He died on the trail in 1852, but other than that nothing else is known about him or the circumstances of his death. 1852 was the year of heaviest traffic on the trail and it coincided with the greatest number of cholera deaths. The odds are pretty good that John Hollman was another victim of the disease. A nice granite marker has been placed next to the road but his original headstone is in the brush somewhere behind a fence. I've seen old photographs of the headstone but I wasn't able to spot it in the tall grass at the time.

I had planned to stay on the south side of the North Platte River but after riding six miles on the unpaved county road I lost my motivation to continue along that route. Back home our unpaved roads are usually hard packed and fairly easy to ride upon. In this part of Nebraska, though, it's like riding on a beach. Fatter tires may have helped but my two inch tires were sliding all over the place. I decided to delve into Mormonism for a while so I could ride on their side of the river. As I've said before, the Mormon National Historic Trail officially follows the north side, and the Oregon National Historic Trail stays on the south bank. In emigrant days both sides had advantages and disadvantages but presently only the north side is paved. That was all the incentive I needed.

On Nebraska Highway 92, I found evidence the area really did have rattlesnakes. Within 20 miles I saw four of them plastered to the pavement. All were prairie rattlers (*Crotalus viridus*). No other species were seen, venomous or not. Pronghorn antelope were also starting to make their appearance. Then I came upon an unexpected landmark, Frog Rock. According to the sign at the turnout, a Mormon pioneer by the name of William Clayton first imagined the likeness of a frog on the cliff. He also claimed he could see Chimney Rock from the top of Frog Rock.

At Broadwater, I renounced my newfound faith and returned to the Gentile side of the river. (In Mormonism, all non-Mormons are called Gentiles. There's an old joke that says only in Mormonism can a Jew be called a Gentile.) From this point the highway follows along the south bank. It had recently been resurfaced so it was like riding on glass. Halfway between Broadwater and Bridgeport, I came to the marker for the Amanda Lamme gravesite. Her grave is actually on private land and can't be seen from the highway.

Amanda Maupin was born in England in 1822. Her husband, Jack Lamme, was seven years older and a descendent of Daniel Boone. In April 1850, they left Independence and started west for California. On June 23, 1850, Amanda succumbed to cholera. As in other familiar stories, Jack supposedly traveled back to Fort Kearny, purchased a headstone, and then pushed it back to the gravesite in a wheelbarrow. Urban legends are nothing new.

I stopped briefly in Bridgeport for lunch at the local Subway and then made my way to Bridgeport State Recreation Area. Like other similar Nebraska parks, this one left much to be desired. Maintenance and upgrades didn't seem to be priorities. Still, it was a campground and it was conveniently located for my journey. By contrast, I've found that Nebraska's Historic Parks are all top notch.

Monday, June 10th - Bridgeport, NE, to Scottsbluff, NE - 44 miles

I was up bright and early again in an effort to beat some of the afternoon heat. Riding out of Bridgeport, I finally felt I was entering the real west. Up to this point, much of the country I had passed through had been farmland. Wheat fields, corn fields, even bean fields dominated my horizons. But then, off in the distance to the south, I saw Courthouse Rock and Jail Rock. Even they were just a prelude to the day's real star: Chimney Rock. Almost immediately I could see the spire ahead. Of all the natural wonders mentioned in pioneer diaries, Chimney Rock inspired the most descriptions. In the earliest journals it was simply referred to as "the chimney." Before the emigrants arrived

Signal Bluff, on the south side of the North Platte River, gave observers a clear view of emigrants and soldiers moving below. *41.335825, -102.227713*

Chimney Rock, near Bayard, Nebraska, was mentioned in pioneer journals more than any other single landmark on the Oregon Trail. *41.703889, -103.348064*

the local Indians had another name for it. Loosely translated, it meant "elk's penis." For obvious reasons, that name didn't get recorded in many diaries.

I arrived at Chimney Rock National Historic Site at 8:00 a.m. As luck would have it, the visitors' center didn't open until 9:00 a.m. I had heard about a trail that began near the old Chimney Rock cemetery a half mile south of the museum, so I went to have a look. I found the cemetery but not the trail. I wandered around the headstones to kill some time. When I got back to the visitors' center I still had 20 minutes left. Up drove Tim. He was from Michigan and was on a quest to visit as many National Parks as he could in three weeks. We talked for a few minutes. Tim said he had driven 700 miles on the previous day. He then snapped a picture of the main entrance sign, hopped in his car, and drove off. Some people can travel thousands of miles without seeing or learning anything.

One thing I saw while waiting for the doors to open was a sign that read, "Warning, Rattlesnakes are common in this area. Please stay on the sidewalk." I didn't have to be reminded of this. A few years earlier, I visited Chimney Rock with my sons. Boys being boys, they naturally couldn't rest until they saw a live rattlesnake. To their credit, they did stay on the sidewalk. They peered closely at the base of every sagebrush until they finally found one. Staying just beyond striking distance, they got the photos they wanted. Certain things you just don't tell mom about.

Once inside the museum, I was greeted by Loren. He'd been at the park since 1994 and was also a past president of Nebraska's OCTA chapter. Loren and I talked history for a bit. Then I asked him about the hiking trail that went to the base of Chimney Rock. He said the trail wasn't maintained and because of erosion the park staff discouraged people from using it.

As I was heading out the door another cyclist was on his way in. Joe was from the nearby town of Bayard. He told me about riding bikes as a child but then giving them up when he started driving. That's typical. For his 50th birthday his wife bought him a bicycle. He was 72 when I met him and still riding a vintage Schwinn Varsity complete with the original "suicide" brakes. Joe told me he also occasionally rides to the top of Scott's Bluff. He had a 76 year old friend who would always beat him to the top. I hope I'm still pedaling when I'm 76.

I continued on to the town of Scottsbluff. On the east side of town I stopped at another famous pioneer grave. Rebecca Winters was a 50-year-old Mormon pioneer who died along the trail in 1852. Again, it was cholera. What's unique about her grave is the marker. Instead of carving a traditional headstone, a friend engraved her name and age onto an iron wagon tire. In the 1890s, a railroad survey crew found the grave and realigned the tracks so her remains wouldn't be disturbed. A century later the railroad was finally forced to relocate her grave for safety. It was moved a few yards away from the tracks so none of the many visitors would get hit by a passing freight train.

Riding into Scottsbluff, I saw a sign at one of the banks that read "98°F." Even though it didn't feel over 97°, I ducked into a Mexican restaurant for a frozen margarita and some fajitas while enjoying their air-conditioning. Refreshed, I mounted the bike and rode the last two miles to an aunt's house.

Tuesday, June 11ᵗʰ - Rest Day in Scottsbluff, NE - 0 miles

My great-grandfather, on my father's side, homesteaded in western Nebraska in the 1880s. Some of the family still lives in the area. My dad settled in Louisiana after he retired so it's rare that I see

The pioneer grave of Rebecca Winters is unique because her name and age were inscribed onto an iron wagon tire placed at the head of the grave. *41.843199, -103.617119*

my Nebraska kin. A rest day in Scottsbluff gave me the chance to catch up on a few years of family gossip with my aunt Bonnie.

Bonnie and I did the obligatory drive up to the top of Scott's Bluff. This sandstone escarpment is named for Hirum Scott, a fur trapper who died near the bluff in 1828. Many legends surround his death. It's said that Hirum became ill and was abandoned by his fellow trappers. Exactly where he was abandoned varies with the telling of the story. His skeleton was found a year later but even that location is debatable.

Although the Oregon National Historic Trail is managed by the National Park Service, the NPS has built very few interpretive centers along the route. Scott's Bluff National Monument is one of them. An excellent visitors' center and library are open daily. On display is a permanent collection of watercolors by William Henry Jackson. From the parking lot, several hiking trails will lead visitors around and to the top of the bluff. The paved road to the summit is famous for its tunnels. As a kid I remember my dad honking the car horn through each of them. I also remember my mom, from Louisiana, being petrified with the knowledge we'd soon be plunging to certain death over the side of

Robidoux Pass was the original emigrant route through the Wildcat Hills near Scott's Bluff. It was seldom used after Mitchell Pass was opened by the U.S. Army in 1851. *41.814757, -103.850442*

a cliff. The road has become so popular for local cyclists that the park service keeps it closed to cars for an hour or two each morning and evening.

After Scott's Bluff, Bonnie and I drove south into Robidoux Pass. This was the emigrants' original route through the Wildcat Hills until 1851, when Mitchell Pass was cleared. Near Robidoux Pass is a reconstructed trading post. Occasionally during the summer, costumed re-enactors tell the story of the Robidoux brothers, Antoine and Joseph, who operated the post here in the 1840s. Bonnie never knew the site existed. Mitchell Pass gets all the attention these days.

Wednesday, June 12ᵗʰ - Scottsbluff, NE, to Torrington, WY - 55 miles

I left my aunt's home at 6:00 a.m., partly to beat the heat but mostly to avoid the morning traffic. She lives on the north side of town and the Oregon Trail passes to the south. Most people that follow the trail these days go through Mitchell Pass. It winds through the Wildcat Hills just south of Scott's Bluff. Mitchell Pass wasn't suitable for wagons until a road was built through it by the U.S. Army Corps of Engineers in 1851.

I followed the original trail through Robidoux Pass. This was the route taken by the Great Migration of 1843, the Donner Party of 1846, and most of the Forty-Niners rushing to California. Now the road is paved except for about ten miles through the pass itself. As I approached the crest of the pass, I stopped to visit four pioneer graves along the north side of the road. None of the markers have names. Nearby is the skeleton of a wagon that didn't quite make it over the pass either. I doubt it had anything to do with the graves. One more grave on the south side of the road is marked "F. Dunn 1849." He was 26 years-old and yet another victim of cholera.

After crossing through Robidoux Pass, I descended five more miles on an unpaved sandy road. When I finally hit pavement, I felt the unmistakable squish of a flat tire. This was my first flat tire since I left Independence. I knew I was on borrowed time because everyone kept asking how many flats I've had. There's never a great place to have a flat but some places are not as bad as others. This one could have been much worse. As I was pumping air into the tire, in a futile attempt to postpone the inevitable, a truck pulled out of the driveway next to the intersection. Gary asked if I wanted to use his air compressor. Air compressors are always better than hand pumps, so of course I accepted. He showed me the compressor in his barn and told me I could work there in the shade. He couldn't stick around, though, because he was on his way down the road to fix a flat tire on a lawnmower. Naturally my tube wouldn't hold air. As I was digging around in my panniers looking for tools, Gary's wife Barbara came out to the barn with a plate of cookies and a glass of juice. That made everything much better.

Once the tire was removed, I found the culprit. A large thorn had pierced the tire and punctured the tube. I put on a new tube and rolled the old one up for patching later. With the repair made, I rolled on to the town of Lyman. Most of the businesses in Lyman have long since closed. The only choice for lunch was the convenience store at the gas station. Just west of town I crossed into Wyoming. Twenty miles later I arrived at Pioneer Park in the town of Torrington. That was where I pitched my tent for the night.

Thursday, June 13th - Torrington, WY, to Guernsey, WY - 43 miles

It was a perfect day to ride. I had a brisk tailwind that pushed me north and west all day long. Even better, it was cool and overcast until well after noon. My first stop of the day was at the Grattan "massacre" monument. Near here, in 1854, three years of relative peace on the plains came to a violent end. What followed were 35 years of attacks and revenge. News reporting in those days followed a typical pattern: if whites were killed it was called a "massacre," but if Indians were killed it was a "battle." Americans were shocked by what they read in the Eastern papers about the Grattan fight.

On August 17, 1854, an apostate Mormon cow strayed away from its herd and wandered into a camp of hungry Sioux. It was promptly killed by a warrior named Flat Forehead and eaten by him and some fellow Indians. The owner of the cow complained to Lieutenant Hugh Fleming the senior officer at nearby Fort Laramie. Fleming met with Chief Conquering Bear, and the chief offered up one of his own horses as restitution. The Lieutenant and the owner weren't satisfied. They demanded Flat Forehead be handed over to them. Conquering Bear refused, so the negotiations ended in stalemate. Two days later a detachment of soldiers led by a young Lieutenant fresh from West Point, John Grattan, rode into the camp. Grattan had no experience

71

My bicycle gives scale to the Guernsey Ruts. These are the most dramatic wagon ruts visible anywhere along the Oregon Trail. *42.255938, -104.748402*

Register Cliff, near Guernsey, Wyoming, is famous for the thousands of emigrant names carved into the soft sandstone. Many inscriptions are lost every year due to erosion. *42.248444, -104.710447*

with Indians but was eager to prove himself. His interpreter, Lucienne Auguste, was drunk at the time and only barely competent when sober. Predictably, things turned bad quickly. This was no massacre. The soldiers came looking for a fight and the Indians simply obliged. When the dust settled, all 28 soldiers, including Grattan, were dead. Ironically, the only Sioux fatality was Conquering Bear.

Riding further west, I soon crossed the Platte River Bridge. This bridge over the North Platte River near Fort Laramie was completed in 1876. It's a three span iron bridge and remained in service for cars until 1958. Today it's used only by bicycles and pedestrians. The bridge is part of the Fort Laramie National Historic Site. Next, I pedaled to the actual fort.

For the earliest trail travelers, Fort Laramie was the last outpost of civilization. Supplies could be purchased or traded for. Wagon repairs could be made at the blacksmith's shop. Mountain men and friendly Indians were usually camped within sight. At Fort Laramie, the most timid of the emigrants often found excuses to turn around and go home. The majority of the wagon trains stayed for a few days before moving on. The fort was originally a civilian trading post built for the fur trade. In 1849, just in time for the gold rush, the Army bought it and turned it into a military fort. It became one of the most important supply points on the entire Oregon Trail.

I parked my bike and spent a couple of hours sightseeing at Fort Laramie. Some of the buildings are original and others have been reconstructed. The small civilian fort had walls but the enlarged Army post didn't. In the vast open plains it wasn't easy to sneak up on a fort. The Army relied on its superior firepower for protection. The bachelor officers' quarters, Old Bedlam, is the oldest standing building in Wyoming. Ruins of the post's stone hospital are also still visible.

Two miles west of Fort Laramie I came to the pioneer grave of Mary Homsley. The grave is well marked but because it's off the beaten path it's seldom visited. Mary was born in Kentucky in 1824 and married in Missouri in 1841. With her parents and her extended family, she and her husband started west in April 1852. After entering Nebraska she gave birth to her fifth child, a boy. As the wagon train neared Fort Laramie, Mary and the baby got sick with the measles. Their wagon overturned while crossing the North Platte River and both were thrown into the cold water. They were rescued, but their condition worsened. Mary died on June 10th. She was wrapped in her feather quilt before she was buried. Her son lived only a few more weeks. He was buried somewhere near Boise, Idaho.

I approached Guernsey from the south and stopped at Register Cliff. Of the many places along the Oregon Trail where emigrants carved their names, this is one of the more well-known. Thousands of names were once legible, but since it's made of soft sandstone, the oldest names are already gone. Many more fade away each year because of erosion. The urge to leave some tangible trace of our existence is universal. On Register Cliff are inscriptions from every decade since the 1850s. Fences deter, but can't completely eliminate modern additions.

I have another aunt, Florence, who lives in Guernsey. I arrived at her house in the middle of the afternoon. After I unpacked and had a quick shower, she pan-fried some delicious elk steaks for supper. One of her sons, Larry, is retired from the railroad and spends a lot of time hunting and fishing. Her freezer is always well stocked with elk and antelope meat as well as walleye and trout.

Friday, June 14ᵗʰ - Rest Day in Guernsey, WY - 6 miles

My aunt Florence was 83 at the time and had lived in Guernsey for many years. Until my visit, though, she had never seen the famous Guernsey Ruts. So before it got too hot for her, we drove out to the site. The Guernsey Ruts are located on the south edge of town. They are the most dramatic example of wagon ruts anywhere along the entire length of the Oregon Trail. Thousands of wagons were forced by the terrain to cross an area of exposed sandstone. As they did, their iron tires scraped deep gouges into the rock's surface. In some places the ruts are three feet deep or more. The town of Guernsey built handicapped accessible walking trails up to the ruts. My aunt appreciated them.

After leaving the ruts, we drove to the mouth of Warm Springs Canyon on the west side of town. The canyon is on Camp Guernsey, a training area for the Wyoming National Guard. A gate normally blocks access to the site but I had been told there was a phone number on the gate to call for entry. When we arrived, the gate was locked and there was no phone number. About two miles west of the gate is the actual Warm Springs. This was a popular campsite for the pioneers because of the naturally warm water flowing from the ground. It gave them a chance to take a bath and do laundry. I really wanted to see the springs.

We drove over to Camp Guernsey's main gate and were given

directions to the Range Control Office. On military bases, this is the office that coordinates the use of various firing ranges and training areas. They are responsible for keeping the soldiers from shooting each other or running someone over with a tank. It's not as easy as it sounds. When I told them about my journey westward on the Oregon Trail they were not impressed. Nor were they too eager to let some crazy bicyclist go riding across their ranges. Luckily, I had a trump card. I pulled out my Air Force Reserve ID card and started talking "military" to them. They finally softened up and sent a guard over to unlock the gate.

My aunt and I drove back to her house and I grabbed my bike. By the time I had ridden back to Warm Springs Canyon the gate was open. I could see why it was such a popular area for the emigrants. The stream through the canyon is lined with cottonwood and cedar trees. Any shade in this part of the country is valued. A double-track jeep trail made for a great ride. Two miles into the canyon brought me to Warm Springs. I couldn't resist sticking my hand into it to see if it was still warm. I was surprised and disappointed to find it wasn't. Time and geology change. As I rode out of the canyon, I closed the gate and called Range Control to tell them I was clear of the area. Warm Springs Canyon is a fantastic place. I only wish it was more accessible to other trail enthusiasts.

Saturday, June 15ᵗʰ - Guernsey, WY, to Glendo, WY - 43 miles

While reviewing my maps once more, I decided it wasn't worth the trouble to ride 18 miles on dirt roads just so I could stay near the original trail for only a few miles. Either way, I was going to have to cut west as the trail continued northwest. So, as I left Guernsey, I followed the paved U.S. Highway 26 until it almost intersected with Interstate 25. Just before the Interstate, though, I turned north onto a parallel dirt road. After three miles I hit pavement again at Wyoming Highway 319. From there it was smooth sailing for the rest of the day.

Off to my left I could see the Laramie Mountains, but the summit of Laramie Peak was obscured by morning clouds. The pioneers got their first glimpse of the mountains as they departed Fort Laramie. Many thought they were seeing the Rocky Mountains. Little did they realize the Rockies were still weeks away. For most of them, the Laramie Mountains were the first really big mountains they had ever seen. For some, it would be the last mountains they ever saw.

My ride along Wyoming 319 was possibly one of the most scenic rides I've ever done. Lots of rain earlier in the spring made the open range a carpet of lush green. With mountains in the background, I weaved through cedar lined canyons and green valleys. Very bucolic. A few miles south of Glendo, I came to a small rodeo practice arena. Four cowboys were perfecting their calf roping skills. This I had to watch. While one guy pulled a mechanical calf around with a four-wheeler (ATV), the other three would try to rope its hind legs. The calf was operated by a car battery which made him buck and kick. It was ingeniously funny.

I rode into the town of Glendo just before lunch. In fact, just enough before lunch that I had to order off the breakfast menu at the local diner. Spanish omelets, they're not just for breakfast anymore. As I sat waiting for my order, a beat-up old car drove by. On the roof, not the hood, was riding a huge dog. The driver wasn't going too fast, and the dog looked like he had done this many times before. You never know what you'll see in small town Wyoming.

Since it was still early, I debated riding on to Douglas. That would have brought my mileage up to over 70 though. I always prefer to ride fewer miles and have time to enjoy the ride and the destination, so I decided to stick with my original plan. After finishing my meal, I rode the last few miles south to Glendo State Park. It's a nice park, but very spread out. Within the park there are eight separate camping areas. The ranger at the gate couldn't tell me which campsites were still available. I just took my chances and rode into the first camp loop I came to. Fortunately, there were a couple sites still open. I pitched my tent and relaxed for the rest of the day.

Sunday, June 16ᵗʰ - Glendo, WY, to Ayres Natural Bridge, WY - 49 miles

It was cool and calm when I started riding. With relatively flat terrain, I covered the 20 miles from Glendo to Orin Junction in no time. There I found a truck stop café. I paused for breakfast and before I knew it an hour had passed. During that time a northwest wind kicked up. Nothing too bad but it was just enough to keep me pedaling all the way to Douglas. Coasting down the hills was not an option.

I made it into Douglas around 11:00 a.m. I was still full from breakfast so I just grabbed a quick snack for lunch. Then I continued west and eventually ended up on Spring Canyon Road. Even though it's unpaved and hilly, the scenery made it all worthwhile. After eight miles, I hit pavement again and turned south towards Ayres Natural Bridge Park.

Two miles before the park is a nondescript private dirt road leading back to the east. At the end of the road, however, is one of the main pioneer gravesites I wanted to see. I stopped at the landowner's home to ask permission. Rose answered the door and graciously allowed me access to the site. The grave of Joel Hembree is the oldest identified grave on the entire 2,100 mile length of the Oregon Trail. Joel and his family were part of the Great Migration. As the travelers passed here on July 18, 1843, six-year-old Joel was riding on the tongue of his family's wagon. He slipped, and before the wagon could be stopped he was crushed by one of the heavy wheels. He was attended to by Dr. Whitman (recall that Dr. Whitman had linked up with the Great Migration as it crossed the South Platte River in Nebraska), but his injuries were too severe. Joel died the next day. His grave was soon lost and forgotten.

In 1962, a previous landowner was gathering rocks to build a small dam. He found Joel's headstone and grave. Joel's remains were exhumed. Forensic evidence showed that in addition to the abdominal injuries recorded by Dr. Whitman, he also suffered a skull fracture. It was also learned that the boy had been placed on a bed of branches and his upper body covered with a dresser drawer turned upside down. Joel was reinterred next to the grave of a cavalry soldier, Private Ralston Baker, who was killed by Indians in 1867. Both graves are now enclosed by a fence for preservation.

I returned to the ranch house and thanked Rose again for letting me visit the graves. We spoke for a while about the history and about past visitors. Rose said that during the previous year a bus load of Chinese tourists visited the site. She added that six or seven different families have owned the land in the past, but all have felt a responsibility to preserve the graves and share their history. I'm glad so many people feel this way. I topped off my water bottles and Rose gave me a couple of cookies for the road.

A short time later I came to Ayres Natural Bridge Park. This sandstone arch is billed as Wyoming's first tourist attraction. It's located on LaPrele Creek, about a mile upstream from where the Oregon Trail crossed. There are stories of emigrants visiting the arch, but in reality most didn't. It was no easy task to get to the arch from the trail. Legend has it that the local Indians were afraid to enter the canyon near the

The headstone of six year old Joel Hembree. He was part of the Great Migration of 1843, and his grave is the oldest identified grave on the entire Oregon Trail. *42.752171, -105.600461*

arch. Supposedly a warrior was once standing on top of the arch and was struck by lightning; a sure sign of bad medicine.

The small park at the arch was a pleasant find. It was by far the best campsite I had anywhere along the trail. The caretaker, Wilfred, kept the grounds spotless. The county owns the property and it's mainly a day-use area. Only eight campsites are available for overnight guests. Being a Sunday night, only three other sites were occupied. A retired Air Force officer and his family were in one spot. In another site, two young high school girls were on their very first camping trip. They brought a truckload of gear: cots, lanterns, ice chests, and a tent. Unfortunately, what they forgot were tent poles. Wilfred came to their rescue and loaned them an extra tent he had. My neighbors in the next campsite, Carl and Lisa, saw I was camping alone. They invited me to join them for hamburgers from the grill. It didn't take long to fall asleep with a belly full of charred beef and the sound of the rippling waters of LaPrele Creek.

Monday, June 17th – Ayres Natural Bridge, WY, to Casper, WY – 48 miles

The gate to Ayres Natural Bridge Park is normally locked from 8:00 p.m. to 8:00 a.m. When I told Wilfred (the caretaker) I wanted to be on the road by 6:00 a.m., he offered to put a snap link on the gate instead of the usual padlock. Sure enough, I was able to leave the park soon after sunrise.

The wind had shifted directions overnight. I started out with a tailwind that lasted all day. Five miles into the ride I came to Interstate 25. I was a little nervous about riding a bicycle on the Interstate. I'd never done that before. In Wyoming, as well as in some other western states, it's legal because there're often no other options. I strapped on my helmet, not that it would do much good, and braced myself for the new experience. I only had ten miles to ride and surprisingly it wasn't all that scary. With the tailwind I moved right along. When I got to the first Glenrock exit, I left the Interstate and backtracked east a half mile on Tank Farm Road. I had yet another grave to visit.

Alvah Unthank's tale has an interesting twist. On June 23,

The pioneer grave of Alvah Unthank. It's located on private land, but is visible from a roadside turnout. A marker at the turnout tells his story.
42.825869, -105.790260

A replica of a portion of the Platte Station Bridge at Fort Caspar in Casper, Wyoming. *42.837714, -106.371657*

Mormon trekkers, in period costume, ascending Independence Rock. *42.493619, -107.131779*

1850, he carved his name into the sandstone wall of Register Cliff (near Guernsey). Nine days later, his companions carved his name onto a headstone. Cholera had snatched another soul. His grave is on private land with no public access but it's visible from the road. An interpretive marker beside the road tells his story.

I stopped for breakfast in Glenrock. The town is situated at the confluence of Deer Creek and the North Platte River. One notable event that happened here involved the Martin Handcart Company in 1856. As this group of Mormon pioneers made their way towards the new Zion, their inferior quality handcarts began falling apart. In order to lighten the load they decided to abandon their heavy winter clothing and extra blankets. Whether as a test of faith or to discourage backtracking, the leaders of the group ordered everything burned. Later, as they crossed the North Platte near Casper, they were hit by an early blizzard. They stalled for almost a week before trudging on to an area now called Martin's Cove (more on that in the next chapter). Before rescuers from Salt Lake City arrived, one in four of the Martin Handcart Company froze to death or died from starvation.

I had hoped to visit a museum at the site of the Deer Creek Station. When I got there, though, the museum was closed and a "For Sale" sign was on the building. On the way out of Glenrock I passed the Rock in the Glen (from which the town takes its name). During John C. Fremont's exploration of the West in 1842, he and Kit Carson camped near the rock. It's said that many inscriptions are carved into the rock but you can't see them. The Rock in the Glen sits on fenced private property. "No Trespassing" signs have been posted by the landowner, Conoco.

My ride from Glenrock to Casper was uneventful. As I entered Casper from the east, I hopped onto the bike path that starts in North Casper Park. It led me across the North Platte River and to the base of the hill where the National Historic Trails Interpretive Center is located. This Bureau of Land Management (BLM) museum overlooks the city and is one of the best on the Oregon Trail. Since it is closed on Mondays, I went straight to the motel. My ride was officially over another year.

Saturday, June 22nd – After Four Days in Casper, WY...

I always build a few extra days into my schedule to allow for the unexpected. In 2012 I needed them, in 2013 I didn't. After riding into

Casper, I checked into Motel 6. It was conveniently located near the bike path and the price was right. I hate to admit it, but since I travel a lot I've become somewhat of a hotel snob. The last time I stayed at a Motel 6 was during my poor college days. I have to say, though, I was pleasantly surprised by the Motel 6 here in Casper. Yes, the room was Spartan. There were no pictures on the walls or carpet on the floor. But it was spotlessly clean, the water was hot, and the A/C was cold. Also, the staff was super friendly.

On the morning after my arrival, I looked into the possibility of changing my flight home. Rather than waiting until my scheduled flight, I hoped to leave Casper early. I discovered it would cost more, actually a lot more, to change my tickets than to just hang around Casper for four more days. So that's what I did.

The first order of business was to get my bicycle and trailer over to a local bike shop to have it boxed up and shipped home. From there I called Enterprise Car Rental. They picked me up at the bike shop and drove me to their office to get a car. They even gave me a military discount. I like discounts. I spent the rest of the day sightseeing around town. I went to the National Historic Trails Interpretive Center and then drove west to see Emigrant Gap. One of the two main Oregon Trail routes out of Casper (or the area that would someday become Casper) passed through Emigrant Gap. It then turned south towards the Devil's Backbone. The oldest route (and the one I subsequently rode in 2014) followed the North Platte River upstream another eight miles before crossing at Red Buttes. Once on the other side, it went west to the Devil's Backbone. There the two trails joined and continued south towards Prospect Hill.

On my second morning in town, I paid a visit to Fort Caspar. The fort was originally called Platte Bridge Station but was later re-named in honor of Lieutenant Caspar Collins, who died fighting Indians a few miles away in 1865. The fort didn't become a military post until the Civil War. Before that, it was the site of several ferries and bridges built across the North Platte. The first ferry was built by the Mormons there in 1847. After that, most emigrants used this ferry or later ones to cross the river. Travelers who couldn't or wouldn't pay the tolls continued upstream to the original ford at Red Buttes (now Bessemer Bend). Since I was the first visitor of the day, I got the grand tour from the museum's manager, Rick. We went from building to building as he unlocked the doors. He explained when the Army took over the fort, many of the troops were "galvanized Yankees." During

Looking south into the valley of the Sweetwater River from the summit of Independence Rock. *42.493619, -107.131779*

the Civil War, Confederate soldiers were often recruited from POW camps to join the Union Army. In exchange for amnesty, the prisoners agreed to wear a blue uniform and serve on the western frontier. This way they wouldn't be put in the position of having to fight against their former friends. They protected the telegraph lines, the settlers, and the travelers on the trail. Many of these soldiers remained in the West after the war when their enlistments ended.

After I left Fort Caspar, I had lunch with Tom Rea. He's the current president of Wyoming's OCTA chapter. He's also a local journalist, author, and historian. We looked over my maps for the next year's ride and he offered a few suggestions. He also called a friend who was the editor of the Casper Citizen, a local on-line newspaper. I was interviewed about my ride and the article was posted the following day. Alas, celebrity still eludes me.

I got up early the third morning and drove southwest to Bessemer Bend. From there I made a recon of the 28 miles between the North Platte River and Prospect Hill along Oregon Trail Road. The BLM advises travelers on this road to use high clearance vehicles and carry plenty of water. I wanted to make sure it was suitable for cycling. As it turned out, the road was no worse than any other I'd been on so far. It was very remote though. For 28 miles I didn't see another car. I suspected it would be even more interesting on a bike.

My last day was spent on the road between Casper and Sweetwater Junction. I wanted to scout out possible campsites for 2014. Much of the land is public and managed by the BLM. Camping is generally allowed anywhere except in the middle of a road. Without access to water, however, the options become limited. A lot of the land is also owned by the Mormon Church. Luckily for me, they've built camping facilities at the various Mormon Handcart Historic Sites in the area. Sometimes things just work out.

I stopped at Independence Rock. I'd been there before but never had the time to climb it. This time I did. Like Register Cliff, thousands of emigrants carved their names into Independence Rock as they passed by. Unlike Register Cliff, Independence Rock is made of granite. These names won't fade away so easily.

At Muddy Gap Junction I talked with the first two touring cyclists I'd seen anywhere on my trip. Ben and Johanna were from Washington, D.C. They were on their 52nd day of an east to west journey across the United States. As I continued west through Jeffrey City, I passed six more touring cyclists. This stretch of highway is part of the Trans-America bicycle route that extends from Virginia to Oregon. I turned around at Sweetwater Station, but not before getting my first glimpse of the snow-capped Wind River Mountains.

That evening I was invited to a dinner party at Tom Rea's home. I met his family and many of their friends. It was the perfect ending to my stay in Casper.

Over the Great Divide 2014

South Pass. That was the focus of my ride in 2014. It's not a difficult pass. In fact, you hardly even know when you've crossed the summit. But for me, as it was for the pioneers, South Pass was a symbolic victory. No matter the starting point or the destination, almost every covered wagon or handcart that rolled along the Oregon Trail crested the Continental Divide at South Pass.

A short distance beyond Casper, the pioneers left the North Platte River and joined the Sweetwater River. Following the Sweetwater upstream, they made their final approach to the top of South Pass. A roadside interpretive site can be reached by cars driving along Wyoming Highway 28 but this isn't the historic summit. Vehicles with higher clearances can travel on dirt roads and visit the true summit. Most people view it, though, like a frame-shot of a longer movie. They stop, take a picture, and then return to the highway. That's not how I wanted to do it. By bicycle, I could follow the original trail over the divide. A great deal of planning was needed to accomplish this and by doing so it became a goal and a highlight of my trip.

Some emigrants made the mistake of thinking South Pass would be the turning point of their journey. Once on the other side, they thought, it would be all downhill to the Pacific Ocean. The more experienced, and the less naïve, knew better. Many miles of desert lay ahead. Dangerous rivers remained to be crossed. The Blue Mountains and the Cascades were still months away. Difficult challenges awaited the pioneers but at least on the other side of South Pass the waters finally flowed towards their future.

Sunday, June 8th - Corralled in Casper, WY

I flew into Casper from New Orleans and spent the next two days putting my bike together and gathering up all the last minute supplies for the trip. One thing I decided to buy was a can of bear spray. When I visited the BLM office, I was told black bears were wandering down to lower elevations because of the previous long winter. Bears had already been spotted in some campgrounds near Atlantic City, along my planned route.

I was all packed and ready to hit the trail. When I glanced out of the hotel window, though, it was 47°F and drizzling. A quick check of the weather radar showed lots of rain headed to Casper from the north. The forecast was calling for showers throughout the day with the possibility of lightning and hail. That was exactly why I built extra days into my schedule. What concerned me most was that my route out of Casper would be completely devoid of any buildings, houses, bridges, or anything else that could be used for shelter in a storm. Also, about 35 miles of it was unpaved. Exhibiting true undaunted courage, I moseyed up to the reception desk and booked another night. After a nice breakfast, I went back to my room and spent the morning watching re-runs on TV.

At lunchtime, I stuck my head out of the hotel with the intention of walking a few blocks to the golden arches. Rain and a 30 mph north wind greeted me. I retreated. Pizza was only a phone call away. When I told my wife about my decision to wait for better weather, she simply said, "I bet the pioneers wouldn't have ordered pizza."

Monday, June 9th - Casper, WY, to Willow Springs, WY - 39 miles

After a day's delay, I finally rolled away from the hotel at 7:00 a.m. Getting through Casper was easy thanks to the Platte River Parkway, a paved twelve mile multi-use path that follows the North Platte River. I wish Baton Rouge had something like it. As I made my way up and over a small pass south of the city, the famous Red Buttes came into view. This was the choke point on the North Platte for the wagon trains. Rock cliffs on both sides kept the oxen, horses, and wagons from following the river any further. For those emigrants still on the south side, crossing here was their last chance.

The location of the earliest ford is now called Bessemer Bend. The BLM has interpretive markers and a nice picnic area at the site. Two major historical events happened here. In November 1812, Robert Stuart and his Astorians built a cabin nearby. It was the first

European styled structure in Wyoming. They were on their way back east from Fort Astoria, Oregon, with dispatches for John Jacob Astor. The plan was to spend the winter here and move on in the spring. Three days after finishing their cabin, though, they got spooked by the large number of Indians in the area and left. They finally stopped for the winter just east of Torrington, Wyoming.

The second big thing to happen here took place in October 1856, and involved the Martin Handcart Company. Beginning in 1847, the Mormons had built a series of ferries across the North Platte River downstream of Bessemer Bend. Entrepreneurs later built more ferries and bridges which eventually put the Mormons out of business. By 1856, only a single bridge remained: the Reshaw Bridge near today's Evansville. When the members of the Martin Handcart Company reached the Reshaw Bridge, they were too poor to pay the tolls. They continued upstream another five miles to where the original Mormon ferry once crossed. As they forded the river a heavy snowstorm struck. Wet but safe on the other side, they continued upstream another mile before stopping for the night. Two days and eight miles later they arrived at Bessemer Bend.

Back at Deer Creek near Glenrock, the Martin pilgrims had burned all their winter clothing and extra blankets. Now they were in dire straits. They had been on a starvation diet for weeks, their handcarts were falling apart, and now they were freezing to death. When they halted at Bessemer Bend they lost their will to move on. They stayed here for six days until urged forward by an advance party of rescuers from Salt Lake City (Brigham Young had ordered a rescue effort when he was told over 1,000 of his flock were still on the trail). From the time they crossed the North Platte until the time they departed Bessemer Bend, approximately 60 people died from hunger and hypothermia.

Beyond Bessemer Bend my route turned to dirt. I started down Oregon Trail Road, also known as County Road 319. Most of the road is built directly on the original trail or very close to it. The BLM strongly warns against traveling on this road unless it's completely dry. The soil out here contains a high amount of bentonite clay. This material is often used in oilfield drilling muds. It is, as they say, slicker than whale snot when wet. I saw a lot of ruts from cars that tried to drive on it too soon after the prior day's storm. But after baking in the sun for a few hours the road was now as hard as concrete.

The first landmark I came to along this road was the Devil's

Facing north on Oregon Trail Road, also known as Natrona County Road 319, as is passes east of the Devil's Backbone. *42.735877, -106.661009*

Devil's Gate. Here the Sweetwater River cuts an impressive gorge through the Rattlesnake Mountains. Nearby, at Martin's Cove, Mormon emigrants awaited rescue in October, 1856. *42.448696, -107.209971*

Backbone. It's a sharp outcropping of vertical rocks that was especially tough for wagons to cross. At one time many inscriptions could be seen on the rocks. Erosion had taken its toll, however, so I didn't notice any as I pedaled by. My next point of interest was Clayton's Slough. It is a natural spring but because of the alkalinity of the water the emigrants were told not to camp there. The spring is named for William Clayton, the same Mormon pioneer who earlier described Frog Rock in Nebraska. Many thirsty animals died after drinking large amounts of the water. Being the environmental scientist my business cards say I am, I couldn't resist checking the pH of the water. Doesn't everyone carry pH strips with them on vacation? I found the pH to be 9. That's not terribly toxic if taken in small doses. Oxen, however, are not that smart. A big blast of alkaline water into the highly acidic environment of a bovine stomach can yield explosive results. Think about the vinegar and baking soda volcanoes built in elementary school.

My final stop for the day was Willow Springs. This was the first good water supply for the pioneers since leaving the river, so it was a popular campsite. A stage station and a Pony Express station were later built near the springs. When cycling in the back country, I normally carry the equivalent of nine bottles of water. Because of Wyoming's notorious wind and lack of humidity, I drank seven of them between Bessemer Bend and Willow Springs. I knew I wouldn't have enough to get me to the next good water source at Independence Rock. If Willow Springs was good enough for the pioneers, it would have to work for me. I first checked the pH (that's really why I had the test strips with me). It was normal. Then I collected and boiled three bottles worth of water. With the two bottles I still had, I figured that would be enough until the next afternoon. I had hoped to camp on top of Prospect Hill but the day's constant headwind and high elevation drained my energy. I was whipped. I couldn't ride any longer. Like so many travelers before me, I made Willow Springs my home for the night.

Tuesday, June 10th - Willow Springs, WY, to Ranch 66 Campground, WY - 40 miles

It was quiet overnight, too quiet. Camped next to a rare source of water in the desert, I expected many critters to come skulking by in the darkness. They were either very good at skulking or I was too tired to notice. Not even a coyote was heard. Around 2:00 a.m. I stepped out of the tent to "see a man about an ox." The full moon completely lit up the barren landscape. It was amazing.

Three hours later I woke up again and started packing. After a quick breakfast of instant grits and a Clif Bar, I began the long slow push up Prospect Hill. I say push because there was very little riding involved. The gain was about 400 feet over two miles. It's not that big of a hill, but for a flatlander like me it was a challenge. Prospect Hill (called Ryan Hill on modern maps) got its name because it gave the pioneers a good "prospect" of the road before them. It's not so much of a hill as it is a large butte that gradually descends back into the valley of the Sweetwater River.

Ten miles after cresting Prospect Hill, I arrived at Horse Creek. The emigrants knew this little stream as Greasewood Creek. It was near here that the Martin Handcart Company met the main party of rescuers from Salt Lake City. Wagon space was limited so only the weakest got to ride. Everyone else continued to walk. A stage station and a Pony Express station were eventually built here. A couple more miles of riding brought me to pavement again. From the time I started on Oregon Trail Road until I hit Wyoming Highway 220, I saw a grand total of one car in 30 miles. There is no substitute for preparation when riding in such remote country.

At this intersection is a sign for the Pathfinder Ranch. It's named for John C. Fremont, the "Pathfinder," whose maps and guidebooks spurred the westward migration of the 1840s. It was near this ranch that one of Wyoming's darker chapters began. In 1889, two adjacent homestead claims were filed, one by Ella Watson and the other by Jim Averell. This infuriated the local cattle barons who had grazed their herds on open public land for years. One morning that July, six cattlemen arrived at Ella's home to "arrest" her for rustling. A short time later they also captured Jim. After several hours of meandering through the countryside, things came to a head, and both were hanged. Ella is the only woman in Wyoming history to be lynched. She was dubbed "Cattle Kate" by the press, but that's a name she never knew in life. In their rush to sensationalize the story and scandalize her, some reporters confused Ella with a notorious prostitute named Kate Maxwell. Later reports cleared up the mistake but the nickname stuck. These lynchings were a prelude to the infamous Johnson County War of 1891-1892.

Another ten miles down the road brought me to Independence Rock. Thousands of emigrant names are still visible, having been carved into granite rather than sandstone. In 1841 the Jesuit missionary Father De Smet called it the "Great Register of the Desert", noting that many inscriptions already existed at the time. Today, it's a protected Wyoming Historic Site. Visitors are free to hike around the base of the rock or even climb it if they wish. From my own experience, it's a lot easier to climb up than it is to come back down. But the views of the Sweetwater Valley are worth the effort. As I sat in the picnic area eating lunch, about 50 Mormon trekkers were winding their way to the top. They were in full pioneer costume. Each summer thousands of Mormons, young and old, come to the area to visit the landmarks and re-enact the travails of their ancestors.

In the time I took visiting Independence Rock, the wind had grown from a pleasant breeze to a full-on headwind. This made the next few miles even more interesting. As I entered Rattlesnake Pass, I stopped at the grave of Frederick Fulkerson. His grave had been misidentified for many years because of pioneer graffiti. Frederick was just 17 when he died here on July 1, 1847. His name was carved on the rock above his grave but eventually faded away. Another traveler, T.P Baker, passed by in 1864 and carved his name and date above the grave. It's still there. Historians naturally assumed this was his grave. Years later a similar inscription left by Baker was found on another rock a half mile upstream from here. Nothing else is known about Baker, but the story of Frederick Fulkerson's life and death were ultimately discovered in a pioneer diary.

Rattlesnake Pass is the route the wagons followed through the Granite Mountains. As the Sweetwater River cut its own path through the mountains it created a deep cleft in the rocks called Devil's Gate. There was no room for wagons to roll through the gate so they detoured instead through the pass. As they exited on the other side, they came into an area now known as the Martin's Cove Handcart Historic Site. The land was previously part of the Sun Ranch but was acquired by the LDS Church in 1997. They've turned the ranch house and outbuildings into a museum. Each year many visitors, Mormon and Gentile, learn about the 1856 tragedy from the church's perspective. The museum does a good job of telling the story of the Mormon emigration through the area, but glosses over much of the non-church related history. For example, nothing is mentioned about the ranch's original owner, Tom Sun, allegedly being one of the six men involved in the Watson and Averell lynchings. As author Tom Rea explained, when you own the land, you own the story.

The actual cove where it's believed the Martin Company sought shelter from a second winter blast is located just west of the museum. It's on public BLM land, but a 25 year lease allows the LDS Church to develop walking trails and install markers. Visitors often push replica handcarts along the trails. Martin's Cove is one of four similar coves which cut into the south face of the Rattlesnake Hills. Church leaders in the 1930s arbitrarily chose this specific cove and it's been sacred ground ever since. There's never been any physical evidence found that links the exact spot to the sufferings of the Martin Company, but having seen this and the other coves, I think the Mormons got it right. In Martin's Cove alone, a grass covered sand dune formed in the middle. This would have given the desperate emigrants the best protection from howling winds and blowing snow.

The weather turned nasty while I was at the museum. I stuck around until the rain stopped, but the wind never did die down. It took me over two hours to ride the eight miles from Martin's Cove to the Ranch 66 Campground. This campground is also owned by the LDS Church. As I said earlier, summertime brings Mormon youth groups and their leaders to the area to learn church history and participate in

The valley of the Sweetwater River as seen from the BLM Split Rock Interpretive Site. The Oregon Trail followed the south side of the river at this point. *42.454201, -107.545731*

The Sweetwater River near the 7th and 8th Crossings. *42.494312, -108.286178*

handcart re-enactments along sections of the trail. To accommodate the seasonal pilgrims, several LDS campgrounds have been established nearby. By agreement with the BLM, the handcarts are not allowed onto the Oregon Trail until July, so I was one of the few campers there at the time.

Wednesday, June 11ᵗʰ - Ranch 66 Campground, WY, to Jeffrey City, WY - 30 miles

My throat was so dry due to the wind and lack of moisture I almost choked while eating a granola bar for breakfast. No amount of water seemed to help. The wind typically dies down overnight but not this time. When I woke up the flaps on my tent were still fluttering wildly. I knew I was in for a tough ride.

The original trail hugged the Sweetwater River. Between Martin's Cove and Ice Slough it crossed the river four times. Because most of this section of the trail is on private property, I decided to stick to the highway. From Ranch 66 I headed south on Wyoming 220 until I reached Muddy Gap. About the only things at Muddy Gap are a gas station and a convenience store. That's all I needed, though, to

The Upper Monument of Rocky Ridge. *42.462892, -108.437026*

find something a little more palatable for breakfast: honeybuns and chocolate milk.

At Muddy Gap I turned onto U.S. Highway 287 and headed west to Jeffrey City. Along the way the BLM has built another great interpretive site. This one tells the stories of the Sweetwater River and Split Rock. Split Rock was a famous landmark. It formed a natural gun sight from which the emigrants could "aim" themselves towards South Pass. Ironically, Split Rock can't be seen from the BLM turnout. You have to travel a few more miles west.

When I reached Jeffrey City, it was time to call it a day. Three days of battling the headwinds had taken its toll on me. Jeffrey City has been described as a modern day ghost town. Its fortunes rose and quickly fell with the nearby cold war uranium mine. Only a few residents and even fewer businesses still hold on. As most U.S. touring cyclists know, Jeffrey City lies along the Trans-America cross country cycling route. The old Lions Club pavilion on the west edge of town has sheltered many cyclists in recent years. The mosquitoes at the pavilion have a legendary lust for cyclist blood. A single shabby motel once served the weary riders but it had been closed for years. Now a new owner was trying to fix it up. Only three rooms were available and

I snagged one of them. Such are the benefits of stopping early.

Just down the road is the Split Rock Café. The Split Rock is what earned Jeffrey City a place on the Trans-America map. They are famous for their plate-sized pancakes. After I settled into the motel and got cleaned up, I walked down to the café for a late lunch. There I struck up a conversation with an older lady sitting at the bar. She appeared to be one of the handful of residents still clinging on to life in the dying town. I told her about my visit to Martin's Cove and my plans to follow the original trail over Rocky Ridge. She smiled and said, "Ya know, the only thing bad about the Mormons is they think they're the only ones who suffered out here." In a way I understood what she was talking about. At the various Mormon Handcart Historic Sites, almost no mention at all is made of the Gentiles that passed this way. Of the half million people that followed the Oregon Trail across Wyoming, only 70,000 were Mormon, roughly 14%. After lunch I walked back to the motel and enjoyed an afternoon free of the dreaded winds.

Thursday, June 12 – Jeffrey City, WY, to Sage Campground, WY – 35 miles

I didn't leave Jeffrey City as early as I would have liked. The Split Rock Café didn't open until 6:00 a.m., and I wasn't about to skip breakfast. I knew it would be four days until the next town. As I was finishing my pancakes I had the cook make me a couple of ham and cheese sandwiches for the road. When I rolled by the Lions Club pavilion, two touring cyclists waved. They had obviously camped there overnight. With little wind I was finally able to maintain a decent pace. I soon arrived at Ice Slough. After crossing the Sweetwater for the fifth time, the pioneers would turn southwest and follow the east side of Ice Slough. The slough got its name when pioneers discovered that by digging down a foot or so into the spongy bog they would hit a solid layer of clear ice. This was a real treat for parched travelers in a hot Wyoming summer.

It was near Ice Slough that another handcart company ran into trouble. On October 19, 1856, The Willie Handcart Company was hit by the same blizzard that halted the Martin Company at the North Platte River. The Willie Company trudged onward until reaching the Sixth Crossing of the Sweetwater River. The LDS Church has built another visitors' center where U.S. 287 crosses the Sweetwater. It is just north of the historic Sixth Crossing. I got to their visitors' center just before 10:00 a.m. After talking with the hosts for a while, I ate one of my sandwiches, applied a good layer of sunscreen, and topped off my water bottles. Then I set off on my own trek through the desert. I followed the same route used by the Mormon handcart trekkers. From the Sixth Crossing, the youth groups in period dress push handcarts for two days until they reach Rock Creek Hollow. Unlike these pilgrims, though, I made the trip solo.

Beyond the Sixth Crossing, the trail moved away from the river for a few miles. Terrain, however, eventually sent the trail back to the river's edge where two more crossings (the 7th and 8th) had to be made within a half mile. When the emigrants were safely on the west side of the Sweetwater again, they followed it until they were forced up Rocky Ridge. The trail along the river from the 8th crossing to Rocky Ridge is now on private land. This requires the Mormon trekkers (and me) to leave the original trail for a few miles and head to the Sage Campground. Since I was probably the first person to travel the route in 2014, portions of the trail were barely visible. I had my GPS with me, so I knew where I was all the time. The problem was that I sometimes didn't know where the trail was. At one intersection, I missed my turn on the first pass. After about 50 yards, I knew something wasn't right. I backed up to where the trail was supposed to be but didn't see any signs of it. I went 50 yards the other way just to make sure it wasn't hiding anywhere. Nope, I was in the right spot. I waded into the sagebrush on foot and after 10 or 15 yards found the path I was looking for. I retrieved my bike and started back in that direction. Before long I found a rock on the side of the trail with an arrow and the word "trekkers" painted on it. Surely this was a sign!

Sage campground is located halfway between the Sixth Crossing and Rock Creek Hollow. It was built and is maintained by the LDS Church but since it's on public land anyone can camp there. I could have ridden another mile or two and camped at the base of Rocky Ridge but I saw a storm approaching from the south. It's never fun to put a tent up in the rain so I decided to stop at Sage for the night. It was only 5:00 p.m. and there was still plenty of daylight left. The showers ended before they made it to my camp. By dark, the sky was clear again. The almost full moon shone brightly as it rose over a small ridge to the west. I was lulled to sleep by the coyotes.

Friday, June 13th - Sage Campground, WY, to Rock Creek Hollow, WY - 15 miles

Long before the handcart disasters, Rocky Ridge had a bad reputation. It's not that it's a particularly high or steep climb, certainly no more so than Prospect Hill. What made it so difficult for wagons and handcarts was that the trail over the ridge was (and still is) covered with large rocks. This led to many broken wheels and axles, along with broken spirits. At the base of Rocky Ridge, near the Sweetwater River, rescuers finally found the Willie Handcart Company. On October 21, 1856, they began a grueling death march. In sub-zero temperatures, howling winds, and two feet of snow the Mormon emigrants walked over Rocky Ridge to Rock Creek Hollow. It took some of the people more than 24 hours to make the 12 mile journey. Today, LDS members find great inspiration in the faith and determination of their ancestors as they toiled across Rocky Ridge. For the modern trekkers, this is the emotional highlight of their spiritual journey.

From Sage Campground to the base of Rocky Ridge it's only one and a half miles. The unpaved road is not too bad but there are a couple of rough spots. It ends at the Lower Monument on Rocky Ridge. Beyond the monument the road is off limits to motor vehicles for the next three miles. The BLM recognized that ATVs were doing irreparable damage to this part of the trail. Hikers, handcarts, horses, and bicycles are still allowed, however.

For most of the way up and over Rocky Ridge I had to push my bike. A mountain bike with full suspension might be able to do it but my fully loaded touring bike had no chance. I figured if the pioneers could push handcarts over the ridge, I had no right to complain about pushing my bike. In a way, the experience was all the more real. Rocky Ridge is not just one ridge but a series of five ridges; the second and fourth are the most difficult. At the top of the highest crest is the Upper Monument. From there I had a long distance view of the Lewiston Lakes and the basins that surround them. The trail around the lakes was just as difficult as Rocky Ridge, but for a different reason. This is open range. With the later than normal spring, the basins were muddy for a longer period of time. Grazing cattle tore up the trail. Once again I resorted to pushing my bike.

A few more miles brought me to the ruins of the Gillespie Place. This is an old ranch house and barn situated near Radium Springs. Within a short distance I had to ford Radium Springs three times. Each time I had to remove my panniers and carry them across the water. They are supposedly waterproof but they're sprinklers not dunkers. I didn't want to baptize my sleeping bag.

I finally arrived at Rock Creek Hollow. Of the 15 miles I traveled that day, I probably walked 10 of them. It was slow going. The land around Rock Creek Hollow is now owned by the LDS Church but the site and the campground are open to everyone. I was welcomed by Elder and Sister Michelson and Elder and Sister Peterson. They were the summer hosts in 2014. The Michelsons treated me to a sandwich and a Diet Coke for lunch and we exchanged lots of trail stories. Like other LDS missionaries I'd met they knew the Mormon chapters of the emigration story, but not much about the bigger picture. They couldn't believe I had actually brought my bike over Rocky Ridge. After lunch they gave me a personal tour of Rock Creek Hollow. The area is hallowed ground to the Mormons. During the night after crossing Rocky Ridge, 13 members of the Willie Company died there. They were buried in a common grave. The exact location is unknown and it's the subject of a lingering debate among historians. Soon after the initial burial, two of the grave diggers died and were also buried nearby. A few marked graves can be seen in the area but these are of unknown emigrants who died there through the years. They are not related to the Willie Company.

Following my tour of that special place, I was shown a spot where I could pitch my tent. I was also forewarned that very soon there would be 350 Mormon youth from Utah camping next to me for the night. I was invited to join them for a dinner of BBQ beef and beans with all the trimmings. It was an offer I couldn't refuse. When the supper bell rang, they fixed me a plate and I sat down among a group of the adult leaders. While I was talking to one of the ladies, she asked me if I ever felt persecuted as a member of the LDS Church living in South Louisiana. She was caught off guard when I told her I wasn't a Mormon. Everyone around just assumed I was. They were impressed I knew so much about the history of their church and their ancestors. Regardless of what you may think of their theology, I will say that the Mormons I met on my trip were among the nicest and most hospitable people one could ever hope to meet anywhere. And, their missionaries ride bicycles.

The ruins of the old Gillespie Place at Radium Springs. The snow-capped Wind River Mountains are on the distant horizon. *42.449846, -108.509144*

The 9th Crossing of the Sweetwater River near Burnt Ranch. *42.376697, -108.716885*

Saturday, June 14th - Rock Creek Hollow, WY, to Pacific Springs, WY - 24 miles

There was a flurry of activity around camp in the morning. Not only was I packing things away, so were the 350 other campers. The smell of eggs and bacon drifted through the valley. I was invited to join them for breakfast but this time I declined. They wouldn't be serving until 7:00 a.m. and I hoped to be several miles down the trail by then. I thanked the elders for their kindness and said my goodbyes. While climbing the first ridge out of Rock Creek Hollow, I looked back on the masses of Mormon youth. I couldn't help but compare this scene to that of their ancestors in 1856. Soon these kids would be boarding air conditioned buses for a day's ride back to Utah. When the members of the Willie Company left the valley, it would take them another month to reach Salt Lake City. Many more would die along the way.

Just over two miles from Rock Creek flows Willow Creek. The land along Willow Creek is also private but I had gotten prior permission from the landowner to cross it. When I spoke to him on the phone, he told me about a small bridge downstream from the trail that I could use if the creek was too high to ford. I put that information in the back of my mind just in case. Crossing Willow Creek looked easy enough. It was only about 20 feet wide, not more than a foot deep, and not terribly swift. I took off my shoes and socks and stepped in to test the waters. With my first step I sank to my knees in mud. This called for "Plan B". I loaded everything back onto the bike and rode downstream to the ruins of the Carpenter Ranch. It took some searching but I finally found the small bridge. It consisted of two telephone poles covered with planks and was used mainly by hunters on ATVs. Once on the other side, I backtracked upstream to the original trail.

The Oregon Trail between Willow Creek and Burnt Ranch is among the least traveled of any section. As such, it was barely visible in spots. I had to pay close attention to my GPS because many equally faint trails crisscrossed the area. Several small gullies and cattle gates had to be negotiated along the way. In terms of riding, though, it was some of the easiest I'd had in several days. The trail was smooth and hard packed.

I was met at the Burnt Ranch by the owners, Rob and Martha. Their grandson Joe was also with them. The Burnt Ranch is located at the historic 9th Crossing of the Sweetwater River. The importance of the site historically, can't be overstated. At various times between the 1840s and 1870s, many enterprises operated here: a trading post, a Mormon mail depot, stage and Pony Express stations, an Army outpost, and a telegraph office. Here the Seminoe Cutoff ended and the Lander Road began. The Lander Road, incidentally, was the only portion of the entire emigrant trails network designed and built with federal funds. In 1859, Horace Greely (of "Go West, Young Man …" fame) passed this way. Two years later a young writer by the name of Sam Clemens rode through on a stagecoach. His adventures along the trail were later published in the book Roughing It by Mark Twain.

As Indian troubles along the Oregon Trail increased in the late 1860s, this area was abandoned. The remaining buildings were burned by the Indians, giving the ranch its lasting name. Rob told me the current ranch house was built sometime between 1900 and 1920. It was almost torn down but he and Martha decided to renovate it. They still have a wood stove for cooking and heat but electricity is supplied by solar panels. I wondered what the original builders of the cabin would have thought about a house powered by the sun.

While Martha was brewing me a mug of black tea on the stove, Rob told me when he was in his twenties he took a bicycle trip from Brussels to Rome. In Rome he sold the bike for $40.00 and came home. What were the odds of meeting a fellow bicycle tourist living in an old log cabin in the wide open spaces of Wyoming?

As I left Burnt Ranch, I crossed the Sweetwater River only a short distance downstream from where the pioneers made their 9th and final crossing. There I began my approach to South Pass following exactly the same trail as a half million people before me. It wasn't so many generations ago. Just east of the summit of South Pass are two small knolls called the "Twin Mounds." With the mounds in view, I was hit by a sudden storm. These were usually short lived on the high desert, so what I often did was cover myself with a tarp and wait for them to pass. That time was different, though. Instead of rain it was sleet. I did what every good Louisiana boy would do upon seeing sleet in June. I panicked. I rushed out from the safety of my tarp and started pitching my tent. I had no intention of being caught without shelter in the blizzard that was surely to follow. As soon as I was inside the tent, the clouds parted and the sun came out again. The net result of my effort was a muddy tent and a muddy me.

A short time later I made it to the summit of South Pass. Here the Oregon Trail officially crosses the Continental Divide. For travelers prior to 1846, this was the beginning of Oregon country. The elevation is now set at 7,540 feet above sea level but different maps often show slightly different numbers. South Pass was the key to the whole Oregon Trail migration yet crossing it was so subtle that many pioneers didn't realize they had done so until they saw the west flowing waters of Pacific Springs. At the summit today are two stone markers. The first one was placed by Ezra Meeker himself in 1906. It reads simply, "Old Oregon Trail 1843 – 57." The second one was placed in 1916 and commemorates the crossing of the Continental Divide in 1836 by Narcissa Whitman and Eliza Spalding. As I said in the Introduction, historians now know they crossed the divide about 20 miles northwest of this point. Still, it was the thought that counted.

I lingered for a while at South Pass. I wanted to savor the moment. As far as I knew, I was the first bicyclist to cross South Pass by following the original trail. There may have been others, but I haven't found evidence of it. I took a picture of my bike in front of the two markers, not so much for proof, but just to capture the memory for myself. On the far horizon the remnants of the passing storm could still be seen. Before I rode away, I picked up one stone as a souvenir.

The historic summit of South Pass. The stone on the left commemorates Narcissa Whitman and Eliza Spalding, and the stone on the right is Ezra Meeker's original 1906 marker. *42.343129, -108.886972*

From South Pass the trail began to fall towards Pacific Springs. The route became increasingly sandy, so much so that I finally had to hop off the bike and push. I stopped at the ruins of the old Halter and Flick Ranch located on the edge of Pacific Springs. This was the traditional first campsite for the pioneers after crossing South Pass. I made it my camp for the evening also.

Sunday, June 15th - Pacific Springs, WY, to Farson, WY - 30 miles

I spent the night among the ruins of the Halter and Flick Ranch. It sits on private property, but the landowner is very supportive of Oregon Trail fans. The ranch itself was built at the site of the Pacific Springs stage and Pony Express stations. Supposedly there was even a bordello here at one time. Before that, the abundant grass and clear water made the area a favorite pioneer campground.

After dark, as I lay in my sleeping bag, I kept hearing a fluttering sound from outside. It sounded like wings flapping but didn't seem like it was flying around. Eventually I realized it was the vocalizations of a

The morning sun casts shadows on my camp among the ruins of the Halter and Flick Ranch. Before the ranch, the Pacific Springs Stage and Pony Express Stations operated here. *42.335912, -108.940379*

bird called a chukar (*Alectoris chukar*). South Pass is on the eastern edge of their range. I had seen some earlier near Willow Creek but I didn't make the connection right away. All those ornithology classes I took in college finally paid off.

When I woke up in the morning there was frost on my tent and my bike. The thermometer in my tent read 38°F but it must have been colder outside. Emigrants often wrote in their journals about seeing snow in the shaded gullies near South Pass as late as mid-July. Since this was their first camp in Oregon country, many wagon trains rested here for a day or two to celebrate the milestone. The women and children would gather wild strawberries from beside the springs and pies would be baked for the occasion. There is even a report of one pioneer mixing snow with fresh cream and peppermint extract to make ice cream for a 4th of July party at Pacific Springs.

Cold or not, I had to get up and get moving. The wind was calm so I didn't want to waste any time. I had another two mile push on the sandy trail before reaching Wyoming Highway 28. Along the way, I passed a BLM marker overlooking Pacific Springs. I also crossed a small bridge at Pacific Creek. For the pioneers, this was the first flowing water they saw that drained to the Pacific Ocean. For me, Highway 28 was the first paved road I had seen in four days. Where the Oregon Trail intersects the highway, the BLM has constructed a large roadside interpretive area. Six or more panels tell the story of South Pass. From that point the highway begins a gradual descent to the town of Farson. A few miles into the ride, I came to a marker for the "Parting of the Ways." Historians now call this marker the "False Parting of the Ways" because it was later learned that the "true" split between the main trail and the Greenwood-Sublette Cutoff was almost nine miles to the southwest.

The Greenwood-Sublette Cutoff was one of the earliest shortcuts on the Oregon Trail. This route was named for Caleb Greenwood and Solomon Sublette and was first used in 1844. It cut seven days off the trip but bypassed Fort Bridger and included a 45 mile waterless stretch. Wagon trains that consisted mostly of farm families tended to follow the main route but beginning in 1849 the gold seekers were more willing to accept the risks of the cutoff.

I rode into Farson around noon and went straight to the only motel in town. After four days on the dusty trail it was time for a hot shower and a bed. The office at Sitzman's Motel was closed but the café next door was just opening. I went inside, ordered the meatloaf special, and asked about the motel. The waitress, who actually ran the café with her husband, was the daughter of the lady that owned the motel. She called her mom and told her I was looking for a room. The owner, Micky, told her daughter to tell me to just go into room six when I finished lunch. Micky later brought me the key, the TV remote, and a pitcher of ice water when she returned to Farson from Rock Springs. You gotta love small town America.

Monday, June 16ᵗʰ - Rest Day in Farson, WY - 0 miles

I spent most of my day in Farson doing laundry and maintenance on my bicycle. I walked over to the local convenience store and stocked up on groceries, fully aware the next food store was 90 miles away in Lyman. There supposedly was a bar and grill further up the trail in Granger but it seemed to be open only when the owner felt like opening it. I couldn't depend on that. My original plan was to ride 60 miles from Farson to Granger in one day. But strong headwinds almost every afternoon and sometimes even in the morning were playing havoc with such schedules. I suspected it might turn into a two day ride.

Across the street from the motel are several historic markers. The Oregon Trail came right through Farson and crossed the Big Sandy River here. It was also near here where the Little Sandy River joins the Big Sandy that Jim Bridger had his legendary meeting with Brigham Young in 1847. Bridger told Young it was a bad idea to settle in the Salt Lake Basin but nonetheless drew him a detailed map to the area. By all accounts the meeting was cordial but ill feelings soon grew between them. In 1855, Bridger reluctantly sold his fort to the Mormons and high-tailed it out of the area. He believed they were planning to kill him.

Tuesday, June 17ᵗʰ - Farson, WY, to Granger, WY - 60 miles

I was determined not to stay another night in Farson if I didn't have to. It wasn't a bad town, I was just getting antsy staying in one place too long. The morning forecast wasn't too promising but the following day's forecast didn't look any better. I decided to go for it. When I left the motel there was almost no wind from any direction. It was chilly but I warmed up once I started riding. Before long I peeled off the first layer of clothing.

Various markers in Farson, Wyoming, commemorate the crossing point of the Big Sandy River on the Oregon Trail and the Big Sandy Pony Express Station. *42.109496, -109.449688*

A replica of a typical ferry used at the Lombard Crossing of the Green River. *41.880066, -109.807602*

Ten miles west of Farson is Simpson's Hollow. Here one of the few military actions of the Mormon War (1857-1858) took place. Even though both sides fielded uniformed forces, almost all the casualties of the war were civilians. At Simpson's Hollow, Utah Militia surrounded Federal troops and forced them to surrender their supply wagons. All the wagons were burned except one. Without supplies, the Army was obliged to spend the winter at Fort Bridger waiting for re-enforcements before they could march to Salt Lake City. This delay gave time for cooler heads to prevail. An all-out war was averted.

Twenty miles more brought me to the Lombard Crossing of the Green River. That was just one of many spots along the river where ferries were constructed. The Green River was an especially dangerous river to cross. It was wide, deep, and very swift. It's said that during the peak of emigration season at least one person drowned every day. At the west side of the modern highway bridge a small park has interpretive panels and a reconstructed ferry for visitors to view.

From the park I rode south 14 miles. There was still no wind to speak of. It was very unusual. When I turned west, though, I noticed a little northwest breeze starting to build up. By the time I finished this nine mile leg a very cold wind was blowing and it was starting to rain. I stopped to put on my rain suit and gloves and then headed south again. For the first time that year I was able to enjoy a strong tailwind. The road I was on was a private road constructed by a local mining company. The signs read "No Trespassing," but I had spoken earlier with the county highway department and they assured me the road itself was open to the public. County equipment is used to oil the road from time to time. As I was making my way south a truck pulled alongside. He asked what seemed to be an obvious question, "Are you crazy?" Little did he realize I had been asking myself the same thing for the last hour.

East of Granger, I came to the pioneer grave of Daniel Lantz. He was one of the thousands of gold seekers that died on the way to California. His original headstone is gone but the site and the story have been preserved. Daniel was 45 when he left his wife and five children at home in Indiana to find his fortune in the goldfields. On July 12, 1850, he died. According to one of his fellow travelers, Andrew Seaton, he "lived until 9 ½ o'clock a.m. His disease was the bloody flux." We now call this dysentery.

The rain and the temperature continued to fall. By the time I reached Granger my fingers were numb. My wool gloves weren't much help in rain. I had planned to camp in the town's ball park but I went to the Town Hall first to see it there was a better option. There I met Vivian. She suggested that pitching my tent in the back yard of the Town Hall might work better. At least I would be sheltered from the wind. She then made me a cup of hot tea to help me thaw out. Only after I set my tent up did Vivian mention that she couldn't leave the building open at night. I had no access to the restroom inside. Fortunately, the back yard was surrounded by a wooden fence and completely out of sight from the neighbors.

Wednesday, June 18ᵗʰ – Granger, WY, to Lyman, WY – 31 miles

It drizzled all night long and by sunrise it was very, very cold. The buttes surrounding Granger even got a dusting of snow. I was nice and toasty in my sleeping bag and I wasn't in too big of a rush to unzip it, but I could tell it was calm outside. In Wyoming, calm trumps everything. I reluctantly started packing. Just across the street from the Town Hall is an original stone Pony Express and stage station. Even though it's on the National Register of Historic Places, it seemed neglected. I walked around the station before leaving town but there really wasn't much to see. Historically, Granger was situated at the intersection of the Oregon Trail and the Overland Trail which came up from Colorado. The station was an important transfer point.

As I left Granger, it was still cold enough that every mile or so I had to stop and warm my hands under my armpits. My gloves were still damp from the day before so they weren't helping much to keep my fingers from going numb. Once the sun came up over the eastern buttes, however, things got better quickly. I followed an unpaved county road heading west. The road was built almost directly on the original trail, and in 1913 it became part of the Lincoln Highway. The Lincoln Highway Association was very much like the Adventure Cycling Association. They didn't build any roads, but they took existing roads, connected them by maps, and published guidebooks for the adventuring motorist. The Lincoln Highway was the first mapped, coast-to-coast motorway in the United States. It predated the Federal highway system by 15 years.

The only natural landmark I passed on the way to Lyman was Church Butte. Grassy flats on the east side of the butte were popular emigrant campgrounds. Most of the traffic that passes Church Butte today are trucks going to the many oil and gas facilities that dot the landscape.

A reconstruction of Jim Bridger's original trading post at Fort Bridger State Historic Site, Wyoming. *41.318621, -110.393408*

I got to Lyman by lunch and found what appeared to be the only open food place, Taco Time. It was a little more expensive than Taco Bell but the food was decent enough. I ate half of what I ordered and put the rest away for supper. A cold west wind had started to blow. I really wanted to visit Fort Bridger State Historic Site but the thought of riding another seven miles into this headwind zapped my enthusiasm. Instead, I rode north out of Lyman and stopped at the KOA (Kampgrounds of America). KOAs are independently owned franchises so you never know what to expect. This one turned out fine. It was going to cost me $26.00 for a tent site but for $42.00 I could get a cabin. I chose the cabin, but pitched my tent next to it to dry in the sunshine.

As I was checking into the KOA, I overheard another group of campers say they were going to eat lunch and then drive over to Fort Bridger. I walked over to their camper and politely asked if they would allow a pitiful bicycle tourist to tag along. They did. Larry, his wife Carol, and her sister Karen had been touring the U.S. for three months in their travel trailer. Now they were on their way home to Oregon.

The main emphasis at Fort Bridger is the period during which the U.S. Army operated it: 1858 – 1890. Tucked away in one corner, however, is a replica of Jim Bridger's original trading fort. Bridger and his partner Louis Vasquez built the fort in 1843 to supply the passing wagon trains. As forts go, this was no prize. But as they say in real estate, location is everything. It was at Fort Bridger that Oregon bound travelers turned northwest, and California and Utah travelers continued southwest. Here, in 1846, the Donner Party chose to take their shortcut to infamy.

While waiting for my new Oregon friends to finish their tour, I struck up a conversation with Jordan. She was a history student from Nebraska doing a summer internship at the fort. We walked through the reconstructed general store she was stationed in and she explained some of the artifacts on display. I learned that a miniature guillotine device on the counter was, in fact, a tobacco cutter. In the middle of the 19th century, U.S. paper money was almost useless in this part of the country. Utah had its own currency that wasn't recognized anywhere else. Tobacco, on the other hand, was valued everywhere. It became the de-facto currency, and tobacco cutters were one method of making change.

Thursday, June 19th - Lyman, WY, to Kemmerer, WY - 42 miles

Riding northwest out of Lyman, I traded the strong headwinds of the past week for strong crosswinds; it wasn't quite as bad. Plus, I had nothing but pavement that day. Ten miles into the ride I came to what used to be the town of Carter. About a dozen houses were still there but it didn't look like any were lived in. Near the train tracks in the center of town stood an old wooden building that looked like every hotel I'd ever seen in a western movie. The front of the building had a square façade and a balcony above the raised porch. I could just imagine dance hall girls on the balcony waiving to passing cowboys below. Oh, the stories their ghosts could tell.

Just before hitting U.S Highway 189, I passed through an opening between two sharp ridges. The gap was named Cumberland Gap by early settlers because it reminded them of the more famous gap in the Appalachians. At the intersection, I turned north and headed towards Kemmerer. From there it was a series of short, steep hills after another. I stopped for a few minutes to watch what I thought were wild horses. Then a cowboy and two cattle dogs appeared from over the horizon and herded them back to wherever. The horses were obviously not as wild as I imagined; another delusion shattered.

An abandoned hotel in the almost abandoned town of Carter, Wyoming.
41.438048, -110.429125

The start of a long, long descent heading west from Kemmerer, Wyoming.
41.806682, -110.606524

It was 1:30 p.m. when I made it to Kemmerer. I was hot and starving so I pulled into the Pizza Hut for a late lunch. I cooled down in their air conditioned dining room for an hour before riding on. Downtown, I passed Kemmerer's biggest claim to fame: the very first JC Penney store was established here in 1902. It's still a working store but there's also a small museum inside. I wasn't interested enough to stop.

Kemmerer is not a large town so it didn't take long to find the town hall. Next to it is a public campground. I think it's mainly used when the county fair is going on. There're only 10 or 12 tent sites and a couple of porta-potties but the price was right so I stopped for the night.

Friday, June 20th - Kemmerer, WY, to Cokeville, WY - 47 miles

Of all the different kinds of places I camp at when traveling, town parks are usually my least favorite. Entry into a state park or private campground is usually controlled in some way. This provides some degree of security. When I'm out in the middle of the desert the security comes from the remoteness of the area. The odds of somebody finding my camp in the dark are pretty slim. But in a town park, everything is in full view and easily accessible. Overnight in Kemmerer I kept waking up, imagining someone was messing with my bike or my gear. I could hear other people coming and going through the park until very late. Being the weekend didn't help. I was glad when morning finally came.

The first five miles out of Kemmerer was a gradual climb. All of a sudden, I crested a ridge. For the next 40 miles it was either downhill or flat. I finally got to use some of that elevation I paid for the day before. Ten miles west of town I came to Fossil Butte National Monument. It looked like an interesting place but the visitors' center didn't open until 9:00 a.m. I wasn't willing to wait an hour and a half.

Twenty-six miles into the day, I entered the Bear River valley. That's where I reconnected with the original trail. On the previous day, after I had passed through Cumberland Gap, I turned north. The Oregon Trail, however, continued diagonally to the northwest. No modern roads or trails follow the original route so I had to detour up through Kemmerer. For the pioneers, reaching this valley meant relief from the parched landscape of western Wyoming. Lush grass and clean water was here for the taking. Today, much of the Bear River valley is protected and managed as the Cokeville Meadows National Wildlife Refuge. The first thing I saw when I rode up to the roadside kiosk was a dead badger. I'd seen plenty of dead prairie dogs, dead rabbits, dead skunks, and even a dead porcupine on the trail, but that was my first badger. Road kill on a wildlife refuge, how ironic. I was also on the lookout for one of my favorite birds, the yellow-headed blackbird (*Xanthocephalus xanthocephalus*). They rarely visit Louisiana, so I was happy when I eventually saw some among the reeds.

Despite my unrest during the night in Kemmerer's town park, I still planned to camp in Cokeville's park. When I saw it, though, I changed my mind. Not that it wasn't clean, it was. The problem was the railroad tracks that passed right alongside. All day long I had seen freight trains thundering through the valley. I knew there would be no peace in the park. I noticed two motels riding into Cokeville earlier. The first was built of tan cinder blocks. It would have been stylish in Soviet East Germany. The other place, the Hide-Out Motel, was straight out of a Clark Griswold vacation movie. It was decorated with wagon wheels, cowboy boots, and even had a teepee out front. Anyone that went to that much work to achieve "the look" definitely deserved my patronage.

Saturday, June 21st - Cokeville, WY, to Montpelier, ID - 34 miles

Within a block after leaving the Hide-Out motel I passed a nondescript little marker beside the road in Cokeville. If I had been driving I would have missed it entirely. The stone on top of the marker must have been one of the original ones placed by Ezra Meeker in 1906. It was worn smooth now. The base of the marker was added in 1950 according to a bronze plaque. It read, "Old Oregon Trail used from 1812 to 1912. Monument erected by Ezra Meeker."

From Cokeville, I continued riding north through the valley of the Bear River. After so many days among the sagebrush, I was overwhelmed by its greenness. Undoubtedly the pioneers felt the same way. Eleven miles beyond Cokeville I turned west again and entered Idaho. Counting 2013 and 2014, it took me 17 days of cycling to cross Wyoming.

Most emigrants never actually had to cross the Bear River. They did, however, have to ford a number of small feeder streams. One particularly difficult crossing was at Thomas Fork. Wagons were

The west side of Big Hill, looking east from a turnout on U.S. Highway 30 near Montpelier, Idaho. *42.235883, -111.233171*

prone to sinking in the soft mud banks of this creek.

After Thomas Fork, the pioneers faced two abrupt ridges called the Sheep Mountains. As I descended into the valley between these ridges, I saw what looked suspiciously like a SAG (support and gear) stop for a bicycle race. Indeed, that's what it was. I stopped and talked with the volunteers for a while. They told me that at the moment I was in the lead. Looking back to the east I could see the competition closing in. It was time to ride on. I soon approached the second ridge, an obstacle pioneers dubbed "Big Hill." The southern tip of this ridge extended almost into the Bear River, so wagons had no choice but to go up and over it. Engineers blasted away the point long ago. Now, U.S. Highway 30 swings down along the river and back up the other side of Big Hill. Roadside markers tell the story of the hill and of Thomas "Peg-Leg" Smith and his nearby trading post.

In the 1820s, while trapping in the area around Yellowstone, Thomas Smith was shot in the leg by an Indian. Even after the wound became infected, none of his friends would amputate the leg for him. He ended up having to use a butcher knife to start the amputation himself. He cut away the flesh but when he started sawing on the bones he passed out. A fellow trapper, Milton Sublette, finished the task. During the following winter, Smith whittled himself a wooden leg to fit over his stump and became known as Peg-Leg. Two decades later he established a trading post along the Bear River near Big Hill. By 1849, he was reportedly earning $100.00 a day selling supplies to emigrants and gold rushers. Smith was typical of most mountain men of the time. He was not all bad, but he certainly wasn't all good either. The signs describe Peg-Leg as "a friend to the emigrants." What they don't tell you is that in his later years he moved to California and made a living, in part, by kidnapping Indian children and selling them to the Mexicans as slaves.

From Big Hill to Montpelier it was only another seven miles. I stopped long enough for lunch at Subway before riding the last two miles to my campsite at the Montpelier KOA.

Sunday, June 22nd - Rest Day in Montpelier, ID - 6 miles

As campgrounds go, KOAs tend to be a bit pricey. Like most private campgrounds, they cater to the RV crowd. This one at least had seven sites exclusively for tents. I couldn't complain too much, though. The restrooms, the showers, and, in fact, the whole park was spotlessly clean. The staff was super nice. They even loaned me a camp chair to make my stay more comfortable. The campground is located on Montpelier Creek. In pioneer days it was known as Clover Creek. Where the creek met the Oregon Trail, a favorite trail campground arose.

That morning I went into town with the intention of having a real breakfast and then visiting the National Oregon/California Trails Center. To my disappointment, I found that Montpelier had very few restaurants and none of them were open on Sunday. The best I could do was a honey bun and orange juice at the Chevron Food Mart. Fortunately, the Trails Center was open. The museum is built directly on the site of the Clover Creek pioneer campground. Dirt in some of the displays is dirt the emigrants may have actually camped on. The museum was constructed and is operated without any government funding (or strings, as they are proud to say). Within the museum, re-enactors tell the story. As you enter you're placed into a group with other visitors and formed into a wagon train. A "wagon master" then leads you through the exhibits. The main emphasis is on trail life. They tell you what you were expected to pack, what you should leave at home, and what the daily routine of five months on the trail would be like. The re-enactors base their characters on actual pioneer diaries.

After I successfully survived the museum trip to Oregon, I set out to explore the rest of Montpelier. That took considerably less time. Montpelier was originally settled by Mormons in 1863. At first it was named Clover Creek but Brigham Young ordered the name changed to Montpelier in honor of the capital of his home state of Vermont. Downtown there is a monument dedicated to the greatest event in Montpelier's history. The Bank of Montpelier was the first state chartered bank in Idaho. In August, 1896, Butch Cassidy and two members of the Wild Bunch (but not including the Sundance Kid) robbed the bank. A deputy sheriff set out in hot pursuit on a bicycle! He followed the outlaws for a couple of miles into Montpelier Canyon, close to where I was camping, before he finally gave up. If only he hadn't been riding a fixie...

Monday, June 23ʳᵈ - Montpelier, ID, to Lava Hot Springs, ID - 60 miles

During the night another touring cyclist set up camp near me. His bike of choice was a bit different than mine. Neil was touring the West on a BMW motorcycle. He was a recently retired lawyer from Arizona and the motorcycle was a retirement gift to himself. From Montpelier, he was heading to the Grand Tetons to meet up with his son. Neil and I talked for quite a while about touring. Except for the motor, his style of travel was not that different from my own. He had panniers on his bike with a dry bag on top. He used a tent hammock which he said was like sleeping on a cot in the air. I personally prefer terra firma.

Since my quest for the perfect breakfast ended in utter failure the day before, I decided to give it another try. Two miles north of Montpelier is the Ranch Hand Trail Stop. They are famous locally for their 24-hour breakfast menu. Success at last; this was my first real breakfast since Jeffrey City. As I walked out of the place, I smiled when I saw the flag by the road. It was hanging totally limp. I knew it was going to be a good day.

Back on U.S Highway 30, I continued to follow the course of the Bear River through Bennington and Georgetown. Beyond Georgetown the road begins a steady climb for four miles up to Georgetown Summit. To the south I could see the faint tracks left by covered wagons as they were also driven to the top. After reaching the crest, I was rewarded with a 15 mile downhill ride into Soda Springs.

The area around Soda Springs was a great curiosity to the pioneers. Numerous bubbling springs and geysers were found nearby. Many are no longer active, and some of the most well-known springs are now hidden beneath Alexander Reservoir. Hooper Springs, though, is still active. It's located in a small park on the north side of the town of Soda Springs. A stone pavilion was built around it years ago. When I arrived at the pavilion, a group of tourists were visiting. Their minivan had a Mexican license plate and only one of them spoke English. We talked for a long time about their vacation and my trip. The family was on their way to Virginia after having visited California and Oregon. While we were still talking, the kids became fascinated by a snake they saw go under one of the rocks near the spring. Kids are the same everywhere.

Naturally, I had to sample the spring water. I guess it's an acquired taste. To me it tasted like unflavored Alka-Seltzer. The pioneers often mixed syrup or honey with it to make a soft drink. Around the turn of the 18th century (1900), water from Hooper Springs was even bottled and sold as a tonic. It's said that other springs in the area tasted like warm beer.

Back in Soda Springs, I rode over to the cemetery. There is a marker here at what is called the "Wagon Box Grave." For the first two decades of travel along the Oregon Trail, Indian attacks were very rare. Beginning in the 1860s they became somewhat more common. Of the half million people that followed one route or another there are roughly 350 documented cases of death by Indian. One such case occurred here. In 1861, a family of seven was traveling with a wagon train. Some of the family's horses had either strayed away or been taken by Indians. While trying to locate the missing animals, they fell behind the rest of their party. According to George Goodhart, one of the people who found the bodies, it appeared that the family was murdered during the night as they slept. One boy had been shot with an arrow, but the rest had been killed with a knife. Their wagon box was lifted off its chassis and placed in the grave. Then the mother, father, and five children were laid to rest in it and covered with quilts and blankets. The wagon's top sideboards were placed over the box. As the grave was filled in, stones were placed at each corner. No one bothered to record their names.

Just west of Soda Springs is Sheep Rock. It's nothing remarkable to look at but at this spot the Oregon Trail split into three branches.

A sculpture at the National Oregon/California Trail Center in Montpelier, Wyoming. It represents the pioneers' descent of Big Hill. *42.322284, -111.297392*

The main trail to Oregon turned northwest to Fort Hall. A second branch turned south to California by way of Utah. This was the route followed in 1841 by some of the Bidwell-Bartleson party. The third branch, the middle one, was the Hudspeth Cutoff. It opened in 1849 and was used mostly by gold seekers looking for a quicker way to their riches. Since the original trail to Fort Hall now crosses the Fort Hall Indian Reservation, I chose to continue west along the Hudspeth route towards Lava Hot Springs. Trespassing on the Indian reservation by non-tribal members is not taken lightly. Between Soda Springs and Lava Hot Springs I had to cross Fish Creek Summit. In a distance of only two and a half miles, I gained over 600 feet in elevation. It may not sound like a lot but where I live I can go 30 miles in any direction and not gain ten feet. As I approached the summit I began playing the "telephone pole" game. This is where you just keep saying to yourself "if only I can make it to the next pole, if only I can make it to the next pole..."

Most emigrants on their way to Oregon would not have passed through Lava Hot Springs. The 49ers certainly did. Today Lava Hot Springs is a tourist haven. There are many resorts in town and the tourists come to soak and play in the naturally hot mineral waters. On the east edge of town is Mary's Place RV Park and Campground. It was once privately owned but now it belongs to the Bannock County Deputy Sheriffs Association. Proceeds from the campground are used to support various outreach programs. As usual, I was the only tent camper in a sea of travel trailers.

Tuesday, June 24ᵗʰ - Lava Hot Springs, ID, to Pocatello, ID - 39 miles

After breakfast in downtown Lava Hot Springs, I resumed my trek along U.S. Highway 30. Right before Interstate 15, I turned north onto Old Highway 91. This road parallels the Interstate, but has almost no traffic. Both routes lay in the valley of the Portneuf River. I followed this road all the way to Pocatello. As I rode into town, I visited a replica of Fort Hall. The site of the original fort is located on the Snake River north of Pocatello. Since it's now on the Indian reservation, special permission is needed to visit the site. Only a small plaque marks the spot. Nothing of the original fort remains.

Hooper Springs, in the town of Soda Springs, Idaho. This was just one of many mineral and hot springs in the area visited by trail travelers. *42.678991, -111.603741*

Reconstructed Fort Hall in Pocatello, Idaho. Nothing is left of the original fort which was located 16.3 miles northwest of this spot. *42.844051, -112.420192*

Fort Hall was constructed in 1834 by an American, Nathaniel Wyeth. He hoped to establish a fur trading company in the area. His dreams of empire never materialized. He sold the fort to a rival company, The Hudson's Bay Company (HBC). Under HBC control Fort Hall was enlarged slightly and the original wooden posts were strengthened with adobe bricks and whitewashed. The fort was the last great outpost of civilization the emigrants would experience before moving on to the Columbia River. Since HBC was a British chartered company, they often tried to persuade the wagon trains to divert to California. In the early years they rightly feared that too many American settlers in Oregon would dilute British claims to the region. In 1856, HBC abandoned Fort Hall and it quickly fell into disrepair. The days of the Pacific fur trade were over.

From the Fort Hall replica, I rode the last few miles through Pocatello to my hotel. I didn't realize it when I made my reservations but the new Holiday Inn Express sits on top of one of the biggest hills in town. I ended my day playing the "telephone pole" game again.

Wednesday, June 25th – Pulling the Plug in Pocatello, ID

When I started my ride in Casper 2014, I hoped to make it as far as Twin Falls. What I didn't plan on, though, were the constant headwinds across Wyoming. I arrived in Pocatello a couple days behind schedule. If I continued on to Twin Falls, I would not have been able to get back to Salt Lake City in time to catch my flight home. So I decided to end this chapter of the journey in Pocatello.

Down Beside the Snake 2015

Just as the Platte River defined the path of the pioneers across southern Nebraska, the Snake River led the wagons through Idaho. The Oregon Trail connected with the Snake at Fort Hall, but I rejoined the trail just west of Pocatello at American Falls. From there the Snake River and I gradually descended to Oregon.

Most of southern Idaho sits atop a high desert plateau. Through the ages, the Snake carved itself a deep gorge as it flowed towards the Columbia River. This made things particularly challenging for man and beast even before the days of western migration. Life

In pioneer days, a series of cascades along the Snake River could be heard from miles away. Today, the cascades are mostly silenced by the lake created by the American Falls Dam. *42.776557, -112.875170*

flourished wherever the water could be reached but away from the river the country was barren. For the Indians who scratched their existence from this land the onslaught of thousands of newcomers was immediately felt. It's little wonder, then, why hostilities between the natives and the emigrants erupted here first. On the Great Plains, the Lakota and Cheyenne could move out of the way until the wagons passed. The Northern Shoshone and Bannock tribes of Idaho didn't have that luxury.

As I biked along this section of the Oregon Trail I witnessed firsthand the importance of the Snake River to the settlement of the area. Agriculture thrives near the water. I saw vast fields of potatoes, sugar beets, and alfalfa. The river, once the source of salmon for the native diet, is now mainly used for irrigation and recreation. Today, dams block the salmon from reaching their traditional spawning beds. On the bluffs high above the river, a new crop has taken root: wind turbines. Huge farms harness the ever-present west wind and turn it into energy for growing cities like Boise. Beyond the wind farms, though, the desert appears little changed. I often rode for hours without seeing another house or vehicle. The trail, in spots, looks very much like it did 170 years ago. Only distant power lines grounded me in the present.

Passing into Oregon, the trail and I swung away from the Snake briefly. At Vale, the Malheur River provided temporary relief before another dry stretch back to Farewell Bend. After Farewell Bend, the Snake River was seen no more. I continued to follow the trail up through the Burnt River Canyon before stopping for the year at Baker City, Oregon.

Thursday, June 11ᵗʰ - To and around Pocatello, ID - 8 miles

I flew from New Orleans to Salt Lake City by way of Houston on the previous day. During the flight from Houston, I struck up a conversation with the guy sitting next to me. Tim was a high school teacher from Texas. He and some 500 other teachers and college professors were on their way to Salt Lake City to spend a week grading the Advanced Placement (AP) exams taken by thousands of high school kids the month before. This particular group of teachers was to grade the essay questions in Government, American History, Art, English, and Foreign Languages. Tim taught Government so he planned to spend the entire week reading the answers to a single question on the exam. I asked him if he tended to get more lenient as the week goes along. He said "no," because each teacher had a specific checklist for each question. The closer a student's answer matched the points on the checklist, the higher the grade. So, whenever your child takes an AP test, this is where it all ends up.

I got into Salt Lake City right on schedule. I had about two hours before my bus to Pocatello was supposed to leave so I grabbed lunch in the airport. Like everything else I'd seen in Salt Lake City, the airport was spotlessly clean. One thing that caught my attention was the airport police (the real ones, not the TSA). They got around quickly in the terminal by riding bicycles. I was never fast enough to get a picture of them, though. I also wanted to see if they could ride on the moving sidewalks.

After lunch I walked outside to where the buses load up. I was still an hour and a half early, but there was already a bus in the parking spot. I talked to the driver to see if she was heading to Pocatello. She was. Next, were there any open seats? There were. She added me to her manifest and called her dispatcher to make the changes. This worked out great. I didn't have to sit around the airport and I got to Pocatello earlier than expected.

When I checked into the hotel, my bike and gear were waiting for me. I moved the boxes to my room but I didn't bother opening anything until the next morning. I found most of the stuff was there, but I noticed the top bracket of my front fender had snapped off. It's happened before and I was always able to repair it with some JB Weld. I probably could have fixed it again but the bracket is a small L-shaped piece of metal that was nowhere to be found. It most likely fell out of one of the lifting holes on the side of the bike box. Oh well, it was time for a new fender anyway. Fenders aren't a necessity, but they are nice to have when riding on dirt roads. The front fender keeps much of the dirt and grime off of the chain.

When I had my bike back together I rode into town in search of a new fender. There were three bike shops in Pocatello but not one of them kept fenders in stock. I ate a sandwich at Subway and then rode back up the long hill to my hotel. I must have been in better shape because the climb was not as bad as I remembered it from the previous year. Back in my room, I called ahead to a bike shop in Twin Falls. Epic Ride Cyclery was right along my planned route. I talked to Ryan and he said they had several fenders that should work. I made plans to visit the bike shop as I passed through Twin Falls.

Friday, June 12th - Pocatello, ID, to Massacre Rocks State Park, ID - 40 miles

I'd forgotten how much fun cycling into a 25 mph headwind for six hours could be. The touring gods reminded me as the day dragged on. When I got up in the morning the wind was calm, it was clear, and it was only 62°F. It was a perfect day for riding. But perfection didn't last long. Soon into the ride, as I changed my direction westward, the wind hit me full force. It didn't let up for the rest of the day. And to add insult to injury, I lost my favorite hat: a Tilley. Since I was on a major road, I had taken the hat off to wear my helmet. I tied the hat to the side of the rear rack, but somehow it must have come loose in the wind. I didn't notice until I was about ten miles up the road. I couldn't bring myself to go back and look for it. The only thing worse than riding into a headwind is covering the same miles twice again. Hopefully whoever found my hat appreciated it.

Most of the original Oregon Trail between Fort Hall and American Falls is now beneath the waters of American Falls Reservoir. I didn't reconnect with the trail until I arrived in the town of American Falls. A series of waterfalls there were very impressive in pioneer days. The roar could be heard from miles away. When a dam was built in 1927, most of the waterfalls were silenced under the new lake. A bigger dam replaced the original one in 1978 and today American Falls Reservoir is the largest lake on the Snake River.

Ten miles beyond American Falls, I came to a rest area on the westbound side of Interstate 86. Travel brochures often play up the Oregon Trail exhibits at the rest area but they turned out to be unimpressive. A paved trail, however, led from the rest area into Massacre Rocks State Park. As I rode on this trail, I was able to see some very distinct wagon swales. The trail also followed along the top of cliffs overlooking the Snake River. With all of the dams and irrigation projects on it today, the Snake is only a shadow of the wild river it once was.

A few miles east of Massacre Rocks State Park, a series of Indian attacks occurred in August, 1862. Several small trains were hit over a period of three days and ended with ten white men being killed. The name Massacre Rocks wasn't actually coined until the early 20th century. The pioneers knew this area as Hell's Gate. Two massive piles of boulders on either side of the trail forced wagons to pass through single file. In the 1920s, developers built a resort along the river, but they didn't like the name Hell's Gate. For some unknown reason they thought Massacre Rocks sounded better. The tourists apparently didn't agree. The resort failed within a few years.

While relaxing at my campsite that afternoon, I was visited by two costumed park interpreters. Steve and Mary were hired for the summer to wander through the campground and talk to campers about the history of the Oregon Trail and the park. We spoke for quite a while. I gave them the names of some good reference books about the trail. Later I bought a new hat in the park's gift shop. It wasn't as good as my Tilley, but it would have to do.

Saturday, June 13th - Massacre Rocks State Park, ID, to Heyburn, ID - 51 miles

I was on the road by 6:30 a.m. My hope was to get as far as I could before the wind picked up again. For the first couple of hours my plan worked but by 9:00 a.m. the west wind had returned. It wasn't as strong as the day before yet it was still tiring.

My first stop of the day was at Register Rock. This is just one of many such rocks along the trail where emigrants felt the need to make a lasting mark. Idaho has preserved the inscriptions by enclosing the rock within a chain link fence and putting a roof over it. It's located about three miles west of Massacre Rocks State Park.

My next landmark was Coldwater Hill. This was the last steep climb the wagons had to make before descending into the Raft River valley. Wagon ruts are clearly visible on the east side of the hill. An Interstate 86 rest area sits at the top of the hill but it wasn't accessible from the frontage road I was riding on.

For the earliest pioneers, and for the least decisive of the later ones, the Raft River was the Oregon Trail's off-ramp to California. As the trail evolved through the years other "partings of the ways" developed further east. Once the emigrants passed the Raft River, though, they were committed to going to Oregon. I turned south from the frontage road onto Yale Road and soon came to a marker near the historic river crossing. Today the Raft River is little more than a drainage ditch. It's almost dry by the time it reaches the Snake River a few miles to the north. I continued to follow Yale Road as it swung south and then west to parallel the original trail. When I made the turn west, I rode into the wind again. For the next eight miles I could barely maintain a 5 mph pace.

I was getting hungry by the time I arrived at the first town of the day. Declo was 42 miles from my starting point. As I rode in I didn't see any restaurants. I asked one of the natives and she said the Little Classroom Café was the best place for lunch. I suspect it was the only place but it was great nonetheless. While eating a turkey sandwich I learned some things about Declo's past. First, the town of Declo was originally named Marshfield. When the post office was established at the turn of the century the townspeople learned there was already another Marshfield in Idaho. The town had to change its name. They decided the first five people to walk into the post office would put their names into a hat. Whoever's name was drawn would get the town named after them. Mr. Declo won. Secondly, I learned that the Little Classroom Café was built in 1979 by a former 4th grade teacher at the Declo School across the street. Every year since then the 4th grade class creates a special plate to be displayed on the wall of the café.

From Declo it was another nine miles to Heyburn. Heyburn has built a nice park along the north side of the Snake River. Within the park they've added an RV campground and saved one small patch of grass for tent campers. Since they had an on-site camp host, I found

Shoshone Falls, in Twin Falls, Idaho, is the largest remaining waterfalls on the Snake River. The trail swung away from the river briefly near here, so most pioneers never saw these falls. *42.598830, -114.431611*

the park clean and well maintained. That was my stop for the night.

Sunday, June 14ᵗʰ - Heyburn, ID, to Twin Falls, ID - 44 miles

When I left Heyburn in the morning I really wasn't expecting much. In fact, the first half of the day's ride was downright boring. Then I saw him. Could it be? Yes, another bicycle tourist. This was the first one I'd seen since before Jeffrey City the prior summer. Lou was from Holland. He started in Vancouver, Washington, and was bicycling across the United States. I complimented him on his wisdom to ride west to east. He wasn't following the normal TransAmerica route, though. Lou was headed to Salt Lake City at the time and hoped to end up in Maine by autumn. He had camped the previous night in the small county park at Murtaugh Lake. Most of the other campers were Hispanic and Lou had been invited to eat supper with them. It was his first taste of Mexican food. He said he loved it.

Eight miles west of Murtaugh Lake is the little known historic site of the Stricker Store and Station. The site is on Rock Creek and was a favorite camping area for trappers, explorers, and eventually

Water flows from the basalt cliffs at Thousand Springs, Idaho. *42.747028, -114.842907*

the emigrants. In 1865, a general store was built there and later a stage station. The store had two cellars both of which have been reconstructed. The dry cellar was used to store flour, grains, etc. The wet cellar was for the really important stuff: the whiskey. The Oregon Trail and later the Kelton Road passed within yards of the front porch of the Stricker Store.

From the Stricker Store I rode north to Kimberly and had lunch. After that, it was only a few more miles to the Oregon Trail RV Park in Twin Falls. Like most RV parks, tent camping seemed to be an afterthought. Still, a couple of sites were reserved for tents, so it worked for me. After I pitched my tent and cooled down a bit I was going to ride over to Shoshone Falls for a quick visit. It was only five miles away. The guy in the site next to me offered to drive me there instead. He wanted to take some pictures of the falls and of the big bridge over the Snake River. We went to the bridge first and saw some base jumpers leap from the side. And they call bicycle tourists crazy? The best views of Shoshone Falls are from the bottom of the Snake River Canyon so I was glad I was riding in a car instead of pedaling my bike. The climb back up would have been a killer.

Monday, June 15th - Twin Falls, ID, to Hagerman, ID - 42 miles

I didn't break camp as early as usual because I wanted to stop at Epic Ride Cyclery to check on a new front fender. The shop didn't open until 9:00 a.m. so there was no need to hurry. I got there around 8:30 a.m. and was met by Austin. He went ahead and opened the store for me and we threw my bike up onto the rack. Ryan had set several fenders aside and luckily one was perfect. It was a new fender but had been removed from another bike because the customer didn't want it. People do such stupid things for the sake of "coolness." Anyway, within 30 minutes we had the new fender on my bike and I was ready to roll. I couldn't believe Austin only charged me $15.00. I tipped him another $5.00 for the quick service.

Getting through Twin Falls was much easier than I expected. When I was west of town I turned north from U.S. Highway 30 to get off the busy road and closer to the original trail. I soon came to the point where Rock Creek empties into the Snake River. Remember at the Stricker Store, Rock Creek was just a small stream you could step across. But by the time it connects with the Snake River, Rock Creek cuts a massive gorge into the plateau. This is why the pioneers swung south of the Snake near Murtaugh. They had to cross Rock Creek before it started carving its way back down to the river.

As I turned west again I heard a voice beside me asking where I was headed. I glanced around and saw a young lady, probably in her late 20s, riding next to me. Kasie was visiting in-laws in the area and was just putting some miles on a borrowed bike. As we rode along, I found out she was from Illinois, she was a dental hygienist, and her husband worked for the State (Illinois). All this would be rather mundane except that my wife is from Illinois, she's also a dental hygienist, and I work for the State (Louisiana). Freaky! I halfway expected Rod Serling to step into the road any minute. After riding seven miles together she turned south and I continued west. I kept thinking of Einstein's explanation of the relationship of time, hot stoves, and pretty girls.

I originally planned to camp at Miracle Hot Springs. When I got there, though, it was still early. I had a slight tailwind and I knew it was only another ten miles to Hagerman. I ate a picnic lunch of tortillas and peanut butter and checked my map on my tablet. Then I started down the long hill towards Hagerman.

A few miles north of Miracle Hot Springs, Salmon Creek drains into the Snake River. Once the pioneers crossed the creek they climbed a bluff to the west and began a long dry journey over Black Mesa. At the end of this 40 mile push they arrived at Three Island Crossing. I had originally thought about retracing their steps across the mesa but ultimately decided not to. There were no significant sights to see and the many wind turbines in place on the mesa were obviously put there for a reason. Even Gregory Franzwa, the author of The Oregon Trail Revisited (the bible of trail followers) recommended against it. So I stayed in the valley and followed the river.

I soon came to an area known as Thousand Springs. Through millennia, as the Snake River eroded deeper and deeper into the ground, it cut its way through a network of underlying aquifers. Think of it as Mother Nature digging a ditch and hitting a water line. Many of these aquifers now gush forth from cliffs on the opposite side of the river. I don't know if there were ever really a thousand of them, this may have been 19th century marketing, but they are a sight to behold.

I turned from Highway 30 onto Bell Rapids Road and followed it west for a mile until it came to a small bridge. Near the site of the bridge, in 1852, trappers constructed a crude ferry. It was the beginning of another "shortcut," the North Alternate Route. For the next three

Wagon ruts are clearly visible on this hillside north of the Three Islands Crossing at Glenns Ferry, Idaho. *42.969060, -115.333330*

Inscription Rock, located on private property at the Ditto Creek Ranch. Rather than being carved into the rocks, most of the names were painted on with axle grease. *43.362553, -115.803871*

years most of the trail traffic followed the new path. It was not an easy route and the toxic waters of Clover Creek, near King Hill, took many lives. By 1855, the ferry fell into disrepair and emigrant travel reverted back to the main trail. Also, just downstream from the bridge was Salmon Falls. In the earliest days of trail travel the pioneers would barter for fish the Indians caught at the falls. Dams ultimately caused Salmon Falls to be submerged by higher water levels.

I crossed the old bridge which was closed to cars. Actually, it probably was closed to everyone but the concrete barricades were no obstacle for my bike. I continued on to the Hagerman RV Village to get a campsite. That's where I discovered the unthinkable. My tablet was missing! I must have left it on the picnic table at lunch. I called back to Miracle Hot Springs, but of course they couldn't find it. It wasn't a great tablet but I had all my maps stored on it. I called Verizon and found out that the nearest store to get a replacement was in Mountain Home. That was still two days away.

Tuesday, June 16th - Hagerman, ID, to Three Island Crossing State Park, ID - 32 miles

From Hagerman I followed U.S. Highway 30 north through the Snake River valley. Before long I crossed the Malad River and started the climb out of the valley and onto the plateau east of the Snake. I stopped in Bliss just long enough to get a honeybun and some juice at a convenience store. I also called Verizon to block service to my missing tablet. At Bliss, Highway 30 joined Interstate 84 but I was able to stay on Old Highway 30 and avoid the traffic. Old Highway 30 follows a wide arc of the Snake and passes near King Hill. As I made the curve I crossed a small stream. It was Clover Creek, the source of water that poisoned so many people on the North Alternate route. Historians aren't sure of the nature of its toxicity. It seemed to be something unique to Clover Creek that wasn't present in other nearby waters. Today the area is covered with farms and seems very peaceful. Not much is left of the actual town of King Hill. A few houses were still occupied but I didn't see any open businesses.

Six miles beyond King Hill is Glenns Ferry, the home of Three Island Crossing State Park. Emigrants approached the crossing from the southeast after making their way over Black Mesa. Here travelers had to make a tough choice: they could risk a potentially deadly river crossing and have a better trail north of the Snake, or they could play it safe and stay on the south side of the river but have 125 miles of dry, dusty trail. This latter route became known as the South Alternate Oregon Trail. The water level of the Snake was usually the determining factor. During three decades of emigration about half chose to risk the crossing. Even with the Great Migration of 1843, the wagons in the lead crossed over but the trailing wagons could not. In the few days that separated the two groups, heavy rains had transformed the Snake into a deep, swift, and impassible torrent. The lives of many pioneers were swept away at Three Island Crossing through the years.

After setting up camp at Three Island Crossing, I rode over to a nearby restaurant and tried their coconut chicken for lunch. It seemed good at the time. I returned to camp and went over to the Oregon Trail Interpretive Center. While there, I started feeling queasy. I went back to my tent and laid down for a quick nap. Four hours later I woke up really sick. I was intending to ride up to an overlook on the opposite side of the river to see the crossing as the pioneers saw it but I was in no condition for that now. I thought maybe I had just eaten too much for lunch. For the past few months I'd been trying to eat healthier so maybe my body was just reacting to the sudden massive influx of fried food. I ended up having to ride back into Glenns Ferry and stock up on Tums and Kaopectate. I knew it was going to be a long night.

Wednesday, June 17ᵗʰ - Three Island Crossing State Park, ID to Mountain Home, ID - 32 miles

"You've Got Dysentery!" is a familiar message to players of the Oregon Trail computer game. That was precisely how I felt when I woke up. I shouldn't have pushed it but I wanted to get to Mountain Home as soon as possible so I could replace my tablet. I felt a little better, so I thought I could make it. Initially, I figured I had just eaten too much for lunch the day before. Now I was convinced I had food poisoning. I wasn't able to eat anything overnight and the morning's breakfast made me nauseous. Still, I left camp as early as I could, again to beat the wind and heat.

I hadn't ridden more than a few miles when I started feeling the rumbling. In addition to the usual and expected symptoms of food poisoning, I was also very weak and dehydrated from missing two meals. Even the little climbs were a chore. For months I had been looking forward to riding along the Main Oregon Trail Backcountry Byway. The first ten miles are paved but the remaining 15 are not.

My campsite in a hayfield near Slater Creek. *43.443866, -115.928996*

When I reached the start of the gravel section at Ryegrass Road, I got sick again. One advantage of riding alone in such remote areas is, if you get sick, you can step off the road and do what needs to be done. No one is going to see you and no one is going to care. Discretion and modesty are of no concern.

I decided to stay on the paved road. Jostling around on a gravel washboard road would have only made matters worse for me. Since all of my good maps were now in the hands of a tablet thief, I could only guess as to whether the paved road I was on would connect back to the Interstate. A few minutes later a utility truck drove by (this whole area is dotted with wind turbines). I waved him down and he confirmed that I would hit Interstate 84 in about ten more miles. I was expecting to have to ride the last ten miles to Mountain Home on the shoulder of the Interstate, but Old Oregon Trail Road passed under the Interstate and rejoined Old Highway 30. I followed this route right into town.

In Mountain Home, I stopped for lunch at the first Subway I found. I was finally able to hold some food down. Then I went over to the Verizon store. Jenn set me up with a new LG 7" tablet that was much better than the one I lost. From there it was just a short ride up the road to the Hampton Inn. I had plenty of rewards points available

Looking northwest along the Oregon Trail between Bonneville Point and Boise, Idaho. *43.493783, -116.042564*

so the night's stay was free. Later I was able to keep supper down. The worst was over.

Thursday, June 18th - Mountain Home, ID, to Slater Creek, ID - 36 miles

I started a little later than normal because I expected a short day. I had previously gotten permission to camp on private land near Canyon Creek, but even with my late departure I was there by 9:00 a.m. Canyon Creek or Barrel Creek as it was sometimes called by the pioneers, was one of the most reliable sources of clean water between Three Island Crossing and the Boise River. Thus, it was a very popular campsite. A stage station was built there in the 1860s and is slowly being restored. I visited with the landowner, Stan, for about 45 minutes but I decided it was way too early to stop for the day.

Ten miles further up the dirt road I came to Ditto Creek. This stream was not as reliable as Canyon Creek but water could usually be found by digging into the moist sands. Located on private land near Ditto Creek is another large rock pile where emigrants signed their names. Most of these names were written with axle grease so they're fading fast. It's not visited often because it's not well known. Also, you have to get permission from the landowner first. When I arrived at Ditto Creek Ranch I was hoping to be allowed to camp there overnight. Unfortunately, the owners were away. A Hispanic lady who spoke little English was able to explain to me that the owners would not be returning until evening. She gave me the wife's cell phone number and I called and left a message. By now it was close to noon and getting hot. I planted myself under a shade tree and waited for a return call. The call never came. I moved on at 4:00 p.m.

In 1862, after gold was discovered in the Boise area, wagons started using the Jeffrey-Goodale Cutoff from Fort Hall. One variant of this shortcut followed Ditto Creek. Another variant crossed the small ridge between Ditto Creek and Soles Rest Creek and followed the latter down to the main Oregon Trail. These two variants were only separated by a couple of miles. A stage station, confusingly called the Ditto Creek Station, was later built along the main trail at Soles Rest Creek. It served travelers on all three routes.

As early as 1862, some travelers on the Jeffrey-Goodale Cutoff reported seeing the bleached bones and burnt wagons of an apparent Indian attack near the site of the future stage station. Since not everyone reported it, perhaps it could only be seen by travelers on one of the variants. Accounts vary widely as to when and what actually happened. Most say it was the work of Indians either in 1852, 1854, or 1858. One diarist, in 1864, claimed the attack was by Mormon "Avenging Angels." This group, which officially never existed, was supposedly Brigham Young's secret police. They were charged with dealing with apostates and other enemies of the church. Many assassinations of the day were attributed to them. Could this have been another Mountain Meadows styled incident but without survivors? Probably not but we'll never know. The exact location of the attack has yet to be found. On old maps, Soles Rest Creek is labeled *Soul's* Rest Creek. Maybe this is another clue. (Note: In late 2016, OCTA member Jerry Eichhorst found what he believed to be a massacre site along Ditto Creek. Cadaver dogs and ground penetrating radar confirmed the presence of human remains. Rifle balls were later discovered at the base of some nearby rocks. An archaeological dig will hopefully be forthcoming.)

I continued on crossing one stream and one ridge after another. You may wonder why the pioneers chose such an up-and-down route. The answer is simple: water. If the wagon trains stayed on the flat land closer to the Snake River, water that flowed from the foothills of the

Danskin Mountains dried up before reaching them. They had to stay high enough in the foothills to find even a meager amount of water and grass for their livestock. This meant a series of long climbs and long descents for us all.

At Indian Creek the ruins of another stage station, the Mayfield Station, are still visible. It was built in 1868 but as far as I know there are no plans to restore it. I had hoped to camp near Indian Creek but the only house in sight was plastered with "No Trespassing" signs. I know when I'm not wanted. I rode down into one more drainage basin. This time it was Slater Creek. I knocked on the door of a ranch house and was met by Jeff. After talking for a few minutes, he gave me permission to camp in his hay field another half mile up the road.

Friday, June 19ᵗʰ - Slater Creek, ID, to Boise, ID - 22 miles

I was lulled to sleep overnight by the sound of coyotes howling in the distance. No sounds of civilization were heard at all. It was great. My morning began with a nice long climb out of the Stater Creek basin. It was followed by a couple more dips and climbs. Finally, I reached Black's Creek, the last major drainage system before Bonneville Point. It was the last tough climb of the day.

During his 1833 expedition Bonneville Point is where Captain Benjamin Bonneville supposedly shouted "Les bois, les bois, voyez les bois!" (The trees, the trees, see the trees!) That's how the river, and subsequently the city, got their names. The BLM has built a nice kiosk at the site. From Bonneville Point, the original Oregon Trail now serves as a hiking and mountain biking trail down to the southern edge of Boise. It's very steep and loose in spots. I can't remember the last time I was thrown from my bike but it happened twice as I was riding down that trail. Luckily I wasn't going very fast. In both cases my trailer lost traction and pulled the rear end of the bike along with it. The only damage was to my pride.

It was during the descent that I saw another unusual site. As I started down from Bonneville Point, I noticed a hiker coming up the trail maybe a quarter mile in front of me. As he got closer, I realized this guy was completely nude except for his hiking boots. He smiled and asked me about my bike and my trip. We talked for a minute or two and then proceeded on our separate ways. I often say that the older I get the more libertarian I become. I wasn't offended by his nudity. If some guy is happy hiking naked through the desert, who am I to judge? But

Ward Memorial Park, Caldwell, Idaho. This is the site of the brutal Ward Massacre which occurred on August 20, 1854. *43.677186, -116.608797*

being unoffended isn't the same as being unsurprised. A nude hiker on the Oregon Trail, what would Ezra Meeker have thought?

At Columbia Road, the wide trail turned into a narrow single track. I knew my panniers would snag on every sagebrush I passed so I chose to stay on the pavement. Instead of getting on the Boise Greenbelt bike path and riding it through town as planned, I diverted west. I hit Gowen Road and followed it over to the Gowen Field National Guard Base. Rather than camping in Boise, I was able to get a room on the base. It was cheaper than a hotel and more comfortable than an RV park.

Saturday, June 20ᵗʰ - Boise, ID, to Parma, ID - 48 miles

It was a lot easier to ride through Boise than I anticipated. But then, it was 6:30 a.m. on a Saturday. Most sane people were still asleep. For 20 miles west of Boise there appeared to be one new development after another. My path eventually opened up into farmland in the Boise River valley. I was almost to Caldwell before I came to my first historic site of the day. It's such an important place and I definitely didn't want to miss it. When I wrote about the Grattan "Massacre" two chapters

139

back, I said true massacres by Indians were rare along the Oregon Trail. The Grattan Battle was anything but a massacre. Near the Ward Massacre Memorial Park, however, a horrendous massacre did occur (coincidentally one day after the Grattan Battle).

On August 20, 1854, a large wagon train led by Alexander Yantis was making its way along the south banks of the Boise River. They were heading for the crossing of the Snake River at Old Fort Boise. Most of the train had already crossed the Boise River near Caldwell but a group of 20 people and six wagons had fallen a day behind. Most of this party consisted of the extended family of Alexander Ward, although there were a handful of unrelated stragglers with them.

Shortly before midday, the Ward party turned off the trail. The Boise River was about a half mile north so they moved towards the river to let their livestock graze and drink. As the Wards were "nooning", a Northern Shoshone tribesman sprang from the sagebrush and stole a horse. One of the Ward sons sounded the alarm and the rest of the group moved back to the trail. They thought they could defend themselves better there.

Some 30 to 40 warriors swarmed the wagons and quickly overwhelmed the emigrants. All of the white men were killed in the initial attack as well as one 17-year-old would-be rescuer from the main wagon train. Two young boys, William Ward (age 15) and Newton Ward (age 9) were shot with arrows and beaten senseless, but survived. They managed to crawl into the brush and hide.

The remaining women and children were not so lucky. The Indians captured them and drove them towards the river. Along the way, Mary Ward (age 17) was raped, tortured, and murdered. Further on, Elizabeth Masterson (age 30 and a sister-in-law to Alexander Ward) was also raped and murdered. The rest of the survivors were taken to the Indians' camp on the north side of the Boise River. No one knows what happened to the two youngest boys. Their bodies were never found. The three youngest girls, however, were hanged by their hair over a campfire and burned to death. Presumably their mother, Margaret Ward (age 37), was forced to watch. She was then tortured with a hot iron rod and hacked to death. Surprisingly, it was not the warriors who committed these atrocities; it was the women of the camp.

A couple days later a search party arrived at the site and buried the dead where they had fallen. Remarkably, they found Newton Ward still alive and carried him to safety. William Ward, still clinging to life,

The "unofficial" City Hall of Adrian, Oregon. *43.739501, -117.072015*

was overlooked. He eventually crawled all the way to Old Fort Boise and was re-united with his wagon train. Newton and William both lived to be old men.

An Army detachment later reburied the bones of all the victims in a common grave where the park now stands. The following summer, three Indians were hanged from a gallows constructed over the grave.

They were then buried nearby. The gallows stood on the site for over 40 years to serve as a reminder of the massacre.

The Ward Massacre was a flash point for a series of attacks and reprisals that lasted throughout the next decade. The immediate effect was the ending of the Hudson's Bay Company's (HBC) operations at Old Fort Boise and Fort Hall. Nine years later, in 1863, a large number of Northern Shoshone and Bannock Indians were massacred by soldiers (actually, California Volunteers) led by Colonel Patrick Connor at the Bear River. The number of Indian casualties is debatable. Connor claimed that 224 warriors were killed, but other estimates range from 400 to 500, including women and children. Regardless of the true loss, the event is considered to be the worst massacre of Indians in U.S. history. Given the impact and significance of the Ward Massacre, it's really a shame that such a small, non-descript park is all that marks the site. It warrants so very much more.

After leaving the park, I swung into Caldwell for a late breakfast at Mr. V's Family Restaurant. I was tired of fast food or peanut butter. As I left town, I crossed the Boise River at the same spot the pioneers did. A roadside plaque commemorates the site.

The emigrants continued northwest to Old Fort Boise at the confluence of the Boise River and the Snake River. In Parma there's a replica of Old Fort Boise. For clarity, it's called Old Fort Boise because in 1863 a "new" Fort Boise was built where the city of Boise now sits. This new fort was an Army post whereas the Old Fort Boise was an HBC trading post. The replica was built based on drawings of the original fort but little inside has to do with the HBC's activities (as a side note, in pioneer days it was often joked that "HBC" stood for here before Christ). Most of the exhibits deal with Parma's history. That's understandable since nothing of the original fort remains. It was an adobe structure that was destroyed and rebuilt several times before finally being washed away for good by the Snake River. The Old Fort Boise Museum is staffed by volunteers for two hours a day on Fridays, Saturdays, and Sundays during the summer. I sat and talked with the volunteers, Jim and Francis, for the entire two hours.

Next to the replica of the fort is a town park with campsites. It's not great for tent camping but for one night it was OK. There's a single motel in Parma. It looked fine on the outside but had poor on-line reviews. I pitched my tent and walked over to Boy's Better Burgers for one of the best cheeseburgers I've ever had.

Sunday, June 21st - Parma, ID, to Vale, OR - 37 miles

After a quick breakfast at the Subway in Parma, I started towards my last crossing of the Snake River. The original main branch of the Oregon Trail crossed near Old Fort Boise but there's no way to cross at that site today. You either have to divert north to Nyssa or south to Adrian. I initially planned to swing north but after talking with Stafford Hazelett of OCTA, he convinced me the southern route would be the better choice. According to him, the road through Adrian was more scenic and had less traffic. He was right on both accounts. The southern route also let me experience a few miles of the South Alternate Oregon Trail which, if you recall, was followed by the emigrants unwilling or unable to cross the Snake River at Three Island Crossing. Before I got to the river, however, I passed through the Roswell Marsh Wildlife Management Area. It was interesting to see familiar marsh vegetation and birds all the way up in Idaho.

I was a bit disappointed when I rode over the bridge into what I thought was Oregon. There was no "Welcome to Oregon" sign. This was the last state on my journey and I really hoped to get a picture of my bike in front of the sign. I was later told that this particular bridge over the Snake River is actually 2 ¼ miles west of the state line. I had crossed into Oregon without even realizing it. In Adrian, though, I did get a nice shot of their "city hall." Other towns could learn from Adrian's example.

Heading north out of Adrian, I soon crossed the Owyhee River and passed through the Owyhee intersection. The intersection is pretty much the town. An old stone gas station is its claim to fame. I stopped just long enough to get a Gatorade and fill my water bottles. "Owyhee" is an old spelling of Hawaii. Many Hawaiians came to the Pacific Northwest in the early 1800s to work for the Hudson's Bay Company.

About a quarter mile north of the Owyhee intersection is a historical marker that tells the story of the "Starvation Camp." This is a marker that if I had not known about it in advance, I would have missed it. There is no sign along the road for it. You really have to be watching to find it. The starvation camp was created by the survivors of the Utter-Van Ornum massacre of 1860.

On September 9, 1860, a train of eight wagons and 44 people were attacked by Shoshones on the south side of the Snake River near Castle Butte, about 75 miles upstream from Owyhee. This emigrant party was mostly the extended families of Elijah Utter and Alexis Van Ornum. The opening attack lasted two days, during which 11 emigrants were killed (including Mr. Utter and his wife). The survivors made their way to the Snake and over the next ten days slowly walked downstream to this location. They dug into the banks of the small Owyhee River to hide and await rescue. After two and a half weeks, Mr. Van Ornum decided to take his wife, two sons, and three daughters and move on. With his family went the two surviving Utter boys and a young man named Gleason.

For the people staying behind, things went from bad to worse. Before they were rescued on October 24th by an Army search party, one man died from choking on a fish bone and four very young children died of starvation (hence the name of the camp). As with the Donner Party of 1846/47, the remaining survivors were forced to cannibalize the bodies of the dead in order to live.

A few miles farther north, I came to a BLM kiosk where most of the wagon trains actually crossed the Snake River. Near the kiosk was another sign about the starvation camp. After a brief stop, I continued north and then turned west onto Grand Avenue. Along the way, I passed the point where the South Alternate route rejoined the main trail. The trail then turned northwest along Lytle Boulevard and up through Keeney Pass.

As passes go, Keeney Pass was not that difficult. But because the pass is so narrow, wagons tended to move up it in single file. That resulted in some very distinct swales which are still visible today, especially on the west side of Lytle Boulevard. Near the top of the pass is another great BLM kiosk.

Just before crossing the Malheur River and entering Vale, I came to the pioneer grave of John D. Henderson. I had noticed that marked graves were becoming increasingly scarce. By this point the emigrants would have been on the trail for nearly four months. I think that death had become so commonplace, and supplies so dwindled, the travelers simply had no compulsion or the energy to carve headstones. John's grave was an exception.

In the early 20th century, an elementary student in Vale was assigned to write a report about Mr. Henderson. He got a little creative with his story and the legend soon developed that John Henderson died of thirst only a short distance from the Malheur River. The true cause of death is unknown, but his dying of thirst is very unlikely. By 1853, everyone knew the river was just ahead. Also, the wagon trains had recently either crossed the Snake River or the Owyhee River depending on their route. Water containers would have certainly been filled at that time. But dying of thirst, with water on the horizon, definitely made a better story than dropping dead with one of the many common diseases of the day. Some sources claim that he died of "black measles" (now known as Rocky Mountain spotted fever), but the evidence seems inconclusive. In 1935 John's younger brother, Louis Henderson was interviewed. He stated only that his brother "took sick and died." Nothing more.

Monday, June 22ⁿᵈ - Rest Day in Vale, OR - 0 miles

I ended my prior day's ride at the Vale Trails RV Park. Unlike many RV parks, this one actually had lots of shade and a grassy patch for me to set up my tent. In the evening another two bicycle tourists arrived and pitched their tent next to mine. I don't remember their names but it was a father and his teenage son from California. They were spending ten days on the road and were traveling very light. The dad said they were averaging 80 to 100 miles each day. It didn't sound like fun to me.

Since I had scheduled a rest day in Vale, I slept in late. It was still nice and cool when I awoke so I strolled on over to the other side of town and had breakfast at the Starlight Café. Along the way, I checked out the town's many murals. Vale is very proud of its history. In town roughly 30 buildings have been painted with large murals that depict the people and events of Vale's past. Some of the murals have an Oregon Trail theme but other subjects are portrayed as well.

Vale was the starting point of the Meek Cutoff. In 1845, Stephen Meek persuaded a train of about 200 wagons and 1,000 people to follow him away from the main trail and west along an untried "shortcut." At the time, tensions were up due to Indian attacks along the Columbia River. The prospect of avoiding that area was appealing. Meek had previously been through much of the area west of Vale, but his experience was based on travel with pack animals rather than wagons. For almost four weeks the train (which ultimately split into two groups) meandered through the hills and valleys of eastern Oregon. Finally, they emerged near The Dalles. During their ordeal it's estimated that almost 50 people died. There was a movie a few years ago called Meek's Cutoff. It focused on just a couple of the families, but its portrayal of a long, brutal, and very boring wagon trip across

Alkali Springs, along Old Oregon Trail north of Vale, Oregon. *44.111168, -117.235262*

Old Oregon Trail, looking down the valley towards Willow Springs. *44.218605, -117.262213*

the desert was pretty accurate. Be prepared, though, if you watch it, the ending left a lot of viewers scratching their heads.

After the grand tour of Vale, I returned to my campsite and grabbed my maps for the next day's route. I walked over to the BLM's district office and met with Dan, one of the office's recreation specialists. We went over the maps and he verified that my route would be fine for a bicycle. I spent the rest of the morning doing some needed maintenance on my bike.

I rode back into town and had lunch at Chavelita's Mexican Restaurant. Next, I went over to Vale's public library to catch up on the news, check my e-mail, and enjoy the air conditioning. All in all, Vale was a great little place to visit. They even had bike lanes on the main highway through town. If I had been in a car, I may not have even stopped. You see so much more on two wheels.

Tuesday, June 23rd - Vale, OR, to Farewell Bend State Park, OR - 35 miles

As usual, I rode out of camp as soon as it was light enough to see the road. I headed north on U.S. Highway 26 for six miles until I came to Fifth Street. I turned east, left the pavement, and started my day along the original path of the Oregon Trail.

I soon came to a large valley known as Alkali Flats. At its upper end lies Alkali Springs. Even though the water was (and still is) sulfurous, the lack of any other water in the area made this a regular campground for the pioneers. Like other alkaline water sources on the trail, livestock tended to get sick and sometimes die if they drank too much. A mile and half up the trail is another smaller spring, now called Tub Springs. Both are located near the base of Tub Mountain. Emigrant diaries often spoke of the two springs together so it's sometimes difficult to know which spring the journalists were talking about. Interpretive panels have been placed next to each one by OCTA.

As I was riding, I occasionally saw snakes that had become road kill. After a while, I was lucky enough to find a live one. Jake, as I named him, was definitely not venomous. I didn't have a field guide with me but I figured he was a gopher snake or some species of garter snake. I later confirmed he was, in fact, a gopher snake (*Pituophis catenifer*). Oregon has only 15 species of snakes and just one of them is venomous: the western rattlesnake (*Crotalus viritis*). This is the same snake Midwesterners call the prairie rattlesnake. By comparison, we have 54 species of snakes in Louisiana, seven of which are venomous.

I continued on to Willow Springs, another pioneer campground, and then crossed Willow Creek. That's where my plan fell apart. There was supposed to be an old Jeep trail that led over the ridge between Willow Creek and Birch Creek. The existence of the trail was confirmed by an OCTA member and, if you recall, a BLM representative the previous day. I looked and I looked and I looked some more. No trail. It may have been there once but I sure couldn't find it. My GPS and my maps told me I was in the right place, and there's no doubt in my mind I was, but the trail was nowhere in sight. The abundant rainfall earlier in the year most likely caused the grass to overgrow the trail. The shortcut always did seem a little dubious to me. When I first looked at satellite images of it on Google Earth, it appeared very faint. I had a back-up plan just in case.

I swung south of Love Reservoir and followed Love Reservoir Road until it linked up with Interstate 84. I had to open and close a few cattle gates along the way but typically this isn't much of a problem. The rule when crossing open range is to leave gates as you find them. If they're open, leave them open. If they're closed, close them back

A meteor crater just south of Huntington, Oregon. The bodies of most of the Van Ornum family were found here by LT. Marcus Reno in 1860.
44.333759, -117.245857

after you pass through. Usually these gates have a snap link or a loop of wire to secure them. When I got to I-84, though, the last gate had a padlock. The only thing I could do was unload the bike and trailer and lift everything over the gate. It was time consuming but not difficult. On the other side of the gate was a "No Trespassing" sign. Oops! Altogether this detour cost me four extra miles.

I got onto the shoulder of I-84 and rode three miles north to the Farewell Bend exit. Thankfully, Oregon is another one of those rare states where you can legally ride a bicycle on the shoulder of an Interstate. Farewell Bend was the last campsite on the Snake River for the wagon trains. From there the river bends sharply to the northeast and the terrain closes in tight. Wagons could no longer follow it. The pioneers said "farewell" to the Snake and turned northwest. Even before the migration, trappers and explorers were familiar with the site. Wilson Price Hunt and some of the Astorians camped there on December 22, 1811. Earlier, they had made the mistake of trying to stay with the river and found themselves deep within Hell's Canyon. Even on foot they could go no further. Hunt and his group were forced to backtrack upstream. They spent the night at Farewell Bend before ascending the Burnt River canyon.

Farewell Bend State Park was a letdown. Even with all the history connected to the area, the State of Oregon has done little to interpret it. There's a nice kiosk with informative panels, but there is no visitors' center. The front gate is left unmanned. The individual campsites are okay, but the bathhouse looks like it hasn't been renovated for 30 years. During my stay, it appeared as though the rangers' main job was to move water sprinklers from one patch of grass to another. This is the first state park travelers on I-84 see when they enter Oregon from the east. You'd think the State would try to make a better first impression. I was also surprised by the lack of cell phone coverage. Since the Interstate is less than a mile from the gate, I naturally assumed there would be a signal in the park. I ended up having to ride back out to the highway to get enough bars to call my wife.

At the end of this long day, I was resting on a bench in the shade when Mary, another guest in the park, walked by. We struck up a conversation. I mentioned how unusual I thought it was not to have a diner or convenience store at the Interstate exit near the park. She asked if I had food for supper. I told her all good bicycle tourists have a stash of peanut butter and tortillas just for emergencies like this. Mary then said she was planning to warm up some leftover Thai food

One of the many wagons on display at the National Oregon Trail Interpretive Center near Baker City, Oregon. *44.813902, -117.728533*

she had bought the day before. She invited me to join her for supper. Hmm? Peanut butter or Thai food; similar but not quite the same. It was a tough call but of course I accepted.

Mary was an interesting person. She was a retired nurse and a full-time RVer. With her on her travels were the ashes of her late husband. She said she just hadn't found the right place to spread them yet. Mary was originally from Missouri but she was on her way to Olympia National Park. She was set to begin a full-time summer job as a camp host.

Wednesday, June 24th - Farewell Bend State Park, OR, to Baker City, OR - 50 miles

I hit the road again at first light. I had entered the Pacific Time Zone the previous day so my departure was at 5:00 a.m. instead of 6:00 a.m. The wind howled through the cottonwood trees all night but it was calm when I woke up. I wanted to get in every possible mile before the wind returned. Of all the days of 2015's ride, this was the day I worried about most. Forty of the 50 miles to Baker City were uphill. That was bad enough, but cycling uphill into strong headwinds would have been even worse.

Two miles north of Farewell Bend State Park is a small meteor crater alongside Old U.S. Highway 30. Besides its interesting geology, the crater has a darker history. Earlier I told you about the Utter – Van Ornum massacre. At the Starvation Camp, I said that Mr. Van Ornum took his family and a few other survivors and went ahead to find help. Tragically, they found Indians instead. On the day prior to discovering the Starvation Camp, a small Army detachment led by Lieutenant Marcus Reno found the mutilated remains of Alexis Van Ornum, his wife, one son, the two Utter boys, and Mr. Gleason. They were all lying within the crater. Missing, however, were the four youngest Van Ornum children. It was later determined that two of the girls died in captivity soon after the attack. Two years later, young Reuben Van Ornum was retrieved from the Indians by his uncle. The fate of the fourth child, a daughter, was never learned. One more interesting side note: If the name Marcus Reno sounds familiar, it should. Sixteen years after the Utter – Van Ornum massacre, Major Marcus Reno would play a pivotal and still controversial role in Custer's defeat at the Little Big Horn.

The first town I came to in the morning was Huntington. I stopped just long enough to get a Gatorade for the road and a honeybun for a quick burst of energy. Five more miles up the road brought me to what used to be the town of Lime. When the lime plant closed, so did the town. Riding next to the ruins of the lime plant was unsettling. It resembled any number of mad-slasher movie sets. Zombies were almost certainly watching my every move.

At Lime, Old U.S. Highway 30 merges onto I-84. I rode onto the shoulder but soon found that the inside lane was being resurfaced. I moved into that lane and had it to myself for the next seven miles. I stopped briefly at the Weatherby Rest Area to fill my water bottles and canteens. This rest area is built upon one of the few wide, flat pieces of land in the Burnt River canyon. It was a major pioneer campground but once again Oregon has failed to interpret the site very well for visitors.

I got back onto the Interstate and rode three more miles to the Durkee exit. Durkee is another town that no longer exists. There were still some houses but the post office closed several years earlier. The old school, built in 1912, became the community center. I wasn't sure if they still used it but it seemed to be well maintained. In front of the building, one of Ezra Meeker's original Oregon Trail markers can be seen.

For most of the day, I traveled up through the Burnt River canyon. This was a difficult stretch of trail for the emigrants because the steep canyon walls came right up to the river's edge. Often the wagons had to roll into the stream bed just to have clearance. It's still an impressive canyon but many areas have been widened to make way for the Interstate. As the pioneers came out of the canyon south of Baker City they got their first views of coniferous trees since Wyoming. They were approaching the dreaded Blue Mountains.

By the time I arrived in Baker City, my honeybun calories had been spent. The first feeding trough I found was the Oregon Trail Restaurant. With a name like that, it had to be good. I went inside and had a delicious western omelet (they're not just for breakfast anymore). Then I noticed the Oregon Trail Motel next door. I did a quick Google search on my tablet and found lots of positive reviews, so I checked in. The room was very clean and a great bargain for only $42.00.

After cleaning up and taking a nap, I walked into historic downtown Baker City. The citizens have done a fantastic job preserving and restoring many of the old buildings. I had dinner at Barley Brown's Brew Pub. Along with my Reuben sandwich, I had one of the best dark beers I've ever tasted. It was a local brew. I wish I could remember the name of it.

Thursday, June 25th - Baker City, OR, to Boise, OR - 145 miles by U-Haul

After breakfast, I went on a walking tour of Baker City. Baker City is one of those rare small towns that somehow escaped the homogenizing influences of corporate America. Even near the Interstate there are very few chain restaurants or chain hotels. This leaves plenty of room for local mom-and-pop businesses to thrive. In a lot of the small towns I've seen, when a chain hotel comes in, a two tiered lodging system develops. Travelers willing to pay for familiarity stay in the chain hotels and the locally owned motels devolve into flop houses for meth heads, hookers, and guys wearing wife-beater t-shirts (you know, the type with no sleeves). That didn't seem to be the case here. I saw a number of small, locally-owned motels in Baker City that appeared to be doing quite well. I certainly had no complaints about the Oregon Trail Motel.

Because Baker City doesn't have a commercial airport or a rental car place, my trip home began a little differently. After checking out of the motel, I rode over to U-Haul and picked up a truck. A few weeks earlier I reserved the smallest truck I could, the 10' version. When I arrived, all they had was a 20' truck. They rented it to me for the same price. I felt silly loading my bike and gear into such a cavernous space but you have to do what you have to do.

I drove east of town to the BLM's National Oregon Trail Interpretive Center. I'm glad I drove. From Baker City it's about five miles uphill to the entrance gate. From the gate to the actual museum atop Flagstaff Hill you climb another 370 feet in a half mile. That's roughly a 14% grade! On my bike I would have died. No doubt about it. But my U-Haul truck didn't even break a sweat.

All the way from Independence, Missouri, people kept telling me how great the Interpretive Center was. They weren't lying. The BLM should be very proud of this place. One of the displays that caught my attention showed the numbers of people that followed the Oregon Trail from various regions of the country. Most came from the Midwest (Missouri, Iowa, Illinois, and Indiana). Only a handful came from the Deep South. In fact, according to the 1850 census of Oregon, only 37 people claimed a state along the Gulf Coast as their place of origin. Who knows, maybe I'm the first person from Louisiana to travel the trail.

After the museum, I drove to Boise over much of the route I cycled the day before. I thought about how much our concept of distance has changed in 170 years. It took me less than an hour to cover the 50 miles between Baker City and Farewell Bend. It had taken me about seven hours to do it on a bicycle. But for the pioneers, it would have taken them at least four days, probably more, to travel the same ground. Whether or not that is progress, only the future will tell.

Paradise Beyond the Mountains 2016

It was a cruel twist of geologic fate that the pioneers faced their toughest climbs and descents not at the beginning of the journey, when bodies and spirits were strongest, but near the end. Two mountain ranges welcomed the newcomers to Oregon: the Blues and the Cascades. Neither range compared to the Rockies for sheer elevation but the steepness of the trail more than made up for the lower altitude. For the earliest travelers the difficulties were compounded by the forest. Fallen trees had to be moved and brush had to be cleared. It was a slow and energy draining process. By this time few had an abundance of energy to spare.

Unlike on the open prairie, the path across the mountains, once blazed, rarely changed. As bad as the trail could be in places, it was just too much work to reroute it. The Barlow Road near Mt. Hood was despised by almost everyone who followed it. The alternative, however, a float trip down the Columbia River was even more harrowing.

The mountains also stirred other emotions. After the Donner Party's tragic experience in the Sierra Nevada during the winter of 1846/47, fears of starvation, freezing to death, and cannibalism were certainly on the minds of the travelers. Most wagon trains hit the Blue Mountains in September or early October. Snow was usually not a threat yet but the occasional early dustings inevitably urged the pioneers to quicken their pace. This sense of urgency and anxiety only increased as they approached the Cascades in mid-October.

It wasn't snow that concerned me as I planned my last miles along the Oregon Trail. Actually, the timing of my ride in 2016 was based solely on the flow of the John Day River. Pioneers typically crossed the John Day in October near McDonald, Oregon. Surprisingly, no bridge was ever built at the site. If I was going to ford the river there, I would have to do so when the water was at its lowest level. This, I learned, generally occurs during the first two weeks of September. The river would have been slightly higher when the wagons crossed a month later, but a 2,000 pound wagon was less susceptible to being swept away than a 200 pound cyclist.

As it turned out, crossing the Blue Mountains, fording the John Day River, and ascending Barlow Pass near Mt. Hood were not as difficult as I expected. What gave me the most trouble was the terrain between the Blues and the Cascades. It looked so flat on the map! As I soon discovered, though, the land between these two mountain ranges presented one long climb after another. It was demoralizing to finally get to the top of a 600 foot hill only to realize that after a quick ride down the other side I'd have to fight for the same elevation again, and again, and again. Similar emotions must surely have gone through the minds of the pioneers. Imagine, after months on a long dusty trail, the end so close you can practically touch it, the limits of your endurance still being tested by each remaining mile.

Wednesday, August 31st - Back in Baker City, OR - 0 miles

I returned to Baker City in the reverse order I left it the year before. I flew into Boise, Idaho, and then rented a U-Haul truck to get my gear and myself back to the Oregon Trail Motel in Baker City. After I checked in I was reading some of their pamphlets and learned a bit of trivia about the motel. Way back in the summer of 1968 the western musical *Paint Your Wagon* was filmed at a remote location 50 miles northeast of Baker City. The Oregon Trail Motel was one of the closest motels at the time, so the cast and crew stayed there. Clint Eastwood and Lee Marvin supposedly paid for various renovations. According to the desk clerk, the entire second floor was added to accommodate the movie stars. During filming it was rumored that Eastwood had an affair with co-star Jean Seberg. You can never know how true such rumors are, though. Sometimes they're started by the production companies just to create buzz around the film. Still, I wonder about the stories the walls could tell.

Thursday, September 1st - Baker City, OR, to Grande Hot Springs Resort, OR - 43 miles

I departed Baker City a little later than I normally like. It was

The Grande Ronde Valley, south of Union, Oregon. *45.190308, -117.869984*

The Summit of the Blue Mountains along Interstate 84, near Meacham, Oregon. *45.463083, -118.386200*

51°F when I woke up so I wanted to give the sun time to rise over the eastern horizon. As I was packing for this leg of the trail, I made the conscious decision to leave my heavy sweatshirt and sweatpants at home. Now I was questioning that decision. My rain jacket, however, served as a decent substitute for a wind breaker.

For the first 20 miles my ride and the scenery were great. I was traveling in the valley of the Powder River. Today this valley is more commonly known as Baker Valley. Wagon trains entered the valley about five miles east of Baker City just below Flagstaff Hill. Years before the emigration ramped up, a single tree, the "Lone Pine" (or sometimes the "Lone Tree") stood as a beacon to Indians, mountain men, and other early explorers. It was located along the Powder River just east of where the Baker City Municipal Airport stands today. In 1836, Narcissa Whitman described the tree in her journal as "a solitary tree quite large, by which travelers usually stop and refresh themselves." In 1842, Medorem Crawford saw the tree and stated that he believed it was "respected by almost every traviler (sic) through this Treeless Country." When Captain John Fremont entered the valley in October 1843, however, he was shocked to find the tree "had been felled by some inconsiderate emigrant axe." Obviously a member of the Great Migration thoughtlessly destroyed a landmark that had welcomed visitors to the valley for generations.

North of Baker City, the first town I rode through was Haines. They have a nice little town park that is filled with cabins rescued from the surrounding area. The next town I passed through was North Powder. Here was where my route intersected the Oregon Trail. The original trail route is followed very closely today by Interstate 84. I had a decision to make. I could get onto I-84 (it's legal in Oregon) and ride along the shoulder of the highway to the Grande Ronde Valley, or I could head east and north on some less busy roads. Since I usually avoid riding on Interstates unless it's absolutely necessary, I chose the less direct route.

Four miles east of North Powder I came to a marker for Marie Dorion. Marie was the Indian wife of a half-Indian, half-French trapper named Pierre Dorion. Pierre had been hired as an interpreter for Wilson Price Hunt's 1811 expedition to the mouth of the Columbia River. Marie and her two young children followed Pierre. It was near this site that Marie gave birth to her third child. The child died nine days later but is remembered as the first non-native child born in Oregon.

As I left Marie Dorion's marker I glanced one last time south towards the Baker Valley. Then I started climbing the ridge that separates it from the Grande Ronde Valley. I knew I was in trouble when I saw the rows of massive wind turbines on top of the ridge. For the next three miles I alternated riding and walking. I can do some hills, and I can do some headwinds, but I'm not a strong enough cyclist to do both at the same time.

Still fighting a strong headwind, I crossed over the ridge and slowly rode north down through a beautiful canyon. As I entered the Grande Ronde Valley the winds suddenly ceased. It was like magic. A few more miles brought me to the town of Union.

Union is not a big town but it looked very well kept. Since it was getting to be lunchtime, I stopped at one of the few cafés I could find, Gravy Dave's. I wasn't terribly hungry but I knew the campground I was aiming for didn't have a restaurant.

From Gravy Dave's it was only five more miles to the Grande Hot Springs Resort RV Park. I know a lot of bicycle tourists balk at the idea of spending $25.00 for a tent site but for me it was worth it. In addition to clean showers, the park had a pool that was heated by naturally hot water from nearby springs. I must have soaked in the pool for at least an hour that afternoon.

Just behind the campground is Craig Mountain. As the pioneers approached the Grande Ronde Valley they traveled on the east side of Ladd Canyon. Today, I-84 goes right through the canyon. The high ground on the east side terminates at Craig Mountain. Scars on the hill are still visible where countless wagons, with wheels locked, skidded down into the valley. The valley floor near Craig Mountain was, and still is, very marshy. The wagons stayed as close to the base of the mountain as possible until they were able to swing around the marsh. The trail passed right through my campsite.

The Grande Ronde Valley was often described by the emigrants as one of the most beautiful valleys they had ever seen. Grass and game were abundant in the area. The valley had served as a meeting area for the Cayuse, Nez Perce, Walla Walla, and other local tribes years before the pioneers arrived. The name literally means the "big round" valley. It is surrounded by the Blue Mountains on the south, west, and north, and the Wallowa Mountains to the east. As the Great Migration entered the valley at the end of September 1843, there was some discussion about stopping and settling in the valley. Realistically, however, the valley at the time was just too isolated. It would be another couple of decades before any permanent white settlements were established. The

Looking down into the Umatilla Valley, near Pendleton, Oregon. *45.599361, -118.615876*

Great Migration, though, did leave one of its own in the valley. On October 1, 1843, a Mrs. Rubey died and was buried there.

Friday, September 2nd - Grande Hot Springs, OR, to Emigrant Springs, OR - 37 miles

It was another later than normal start for me. At around 6:30 a.m., I could see rain falling ahead in La Grande. There was no reason to get wet at the start of a day. I just waited until the storm passed and was on the road by 7:30 a.m.

My plan was to grab a quick breakfast at some convenience store in La Grande right before getting on I-84. As I got near the Interstate, however, there were no stores within sight. Since Hilgard Junction State Park was only six more miles up the road, I decided to wait and have a picnic breakfast there.

If you recall from earlier chapters, the 1843 migration was accompanied by Dr. Marcus Whitman. He was a veteran of two earlier crossings on the Oregon Trail and it was with his encouragement that the Great Migration continued past Fort Hall with their wagons. While camped in the Grande Ronde Valley, Whitman received a message from his mission near Walla Walla urging his quick return. He took his leave from the wagon train but left a trusted Cayuse guide named Stickus to lead the emigrants over the Blue Mountains. Before he left, he promised the travelers they could obtain needed supplies at his mission when they arrived.

The 1843 emigrants had a unique challenge not faced by later groups. Being the first to bring their wagons, it fell upon them to blaze a roadway through the forest up and over the Blue Mountains. They had complete confidence in their Cayuse guide but human nature being what it is, the job of actually cutting the trees was shirked by many in their group. The Great Migration started with over 1,000 people. If we assume at least 10% of them were able bodied men, there should have been plenty of available labor to cut the path. Yet, in a fact that didn't go unnoticed in pioneer journals; many found convenient excuses (such as looking for "lost" livestock) to not wield an axe. The hardest work, then, was accomplished by a small team of devoted men.

Through the years, as wagon trains started the ascent up the Blues, they often stopped at Hilgard Junction to camp or regroup. This was a wide spot in the valley of the Grande Ronde River. Today a State Park is located at the site. There's a campground there but I stopped just long enough to eat a couple of peanut butter tortillas and refill my water bottles.

My original plan was to ride on the shoulder of I-84 just until I reached the Old Emigrant Hill Scenic Frontage Road at exit 248. This was four miles beyond Hilgard Junction. When I got to that exit, however, I reevaluated my situation. I normally don't like to ride on an Interstate but I had to admit it was going pretty well so far. The shoulder was wide and unusually clean. I knew that secondary roads typically have steeper grades and I knew there was plenty of climbing ahead. In a spur of the moment decision I opted to stay on I-84 until I approached Meacham. Two miles before the Meacham exit, I crossed the summit of the Blue Mountains (elevation 4,193 feet).

It was shortly after 2:00 p.m. when I reached Meacham. I walked into the Oregon Trail Store and Deli for a bite of lunch. I was immediately invited by the store's owner, Dixie, to join her and another couple at the "community table." Dixie also serves as the town's postmaster. For the next hour she filled me in on the history of Meacham and her store. At one time Meacham had a population of 2,000. It had two sawmills and a stockyard. In July 1923, President Warren G. Harding and his entire cabinet visited Meacham to commemorate the 80th anniversary of the Great Migration. On that day, reporters claimed, Meacham was the Capital of the United States. Less than a month later President Harding died of a cerebral hemorrhage in San Francisco.

Dixie's store was built in 1910 and moved to its current location a year later. Originally, one side of the store was a bar and the other side had a deli. Kids were not allowed to cross a painted line on the floor that separated the two sides. Today the store has become somewhat of a landmark for touring motorcyclists.

Three more miles brought me to Emigrant Springs State Park. The springs themselves were not actually located on the Oregon Trail but were close enough that many travelers veered a quarter mile off the trail to partake of the waters. Ezra Meeker placed one of his markers near the springs. The marker is still visible but construction of US Highway 30 resulted in almost completely stopping the flow of water from the springs.

The park's campground was my stopping point for the night. During the summer rangers give a variety of park tours. Some presentations address the emigrant history but other talks cover the park's geology, plant and animal life, and pre-emigrant Indian history. Signs in the park alert visitors to the possibility of black bear and mountain lion encounters. I was told that no black bears had been seen in a long time but a mountain lion was reported earlier in the summer. No need to worry, though. The biggest threats to the food supply of campers were raccoons and squirrels.

Saturday, September 3rd - Emigrant Springs, OR, to Echo, OR - 52 miles

Leaving Emigrant Springs State Park, I followed Old Highway 30 for six miles until it reached the I-84 rest areas at Deadman Pass. A small access tunnel goes under the Interstate to connect both areas. On the eastbound side a sign directs visitors to some nice wagon swales just beyond a fence. Metal stairs over the fence allow for closer looks.

The route of the original trail crosses the Interstate at this point. Once I finished looking at the swales, I returned to the westbound side and rejoined Old Highway 30. At the rest area this road changes names and becomes Old Emigrant Hill Road. For the first mile it was a relatively easy 200 foot climb. Then the fun began. For the next 12 miles I had the road to myself. It had recently been resurfaced so it was nice and smooth. In those 12 miles I dropped almost 2,000 feet in elevation. My hands were getting sore gripping the handlebars and squeezing the brakes. It was the best downhill ride I've ever had. The scenery was absolutely amazing!

Through the valley flows the Umatilla River. The wagon trains actually struck the river four miles above where I approached it. If you think of the Oregon Trail as a braided rope, the Umatilla River is where the braids began to unravel. In the earliest years the emigrants would travel three miles downstream, cross the river, and make a beeline for the Walla Walla River. There they would visit either the Whitman Mission or the Hudson's Bay Company's post at the confluence of the Walla Walla and the Columbia River. Since the land between the Umatilla and the Walla Walla was wide open country, the wagons would spread out. If distinct traces were ever visible, they were long ago erased by plows.

All of the 1843 wagons went to the Walla Walla. Some, such as the Applegate clan, built boats and continued their journey on the Columbia. Others kept their wagons intact and followed the Columbia's

Then as now, Well Springs was often a crusted over mud flat. *45.632306, -119.706822*

south bank. In 1844, Moses "Black" Harris guided a small group down the Umatilla River to its mouth at the Columbia. Gradually, fewer and fewer travelers made the detour to the Walla Walla. After the massacre at the Whitman Mission in 1847, most pioneers steered clear of the Columbia as long as possible.

The preferred route eventually settled on a crossing of the Umatilla River at present-day Pendleton (the Upper Crossing). From there it went to the high ground and followed the bluffs of the river until dropping back down into the valley at Corral Springs.

I got to Pendleton in time for lunch. I won't say the name of the place I ate at since I wasn't very impressed with it. The food was fine but the atmosphere was a letdown. Have you ever walked into a place and just felt like you didn't belong? All of the patrons seemed to know each other. I wasn't a regular so no one bothered to smile or say "hello." Of all the cafés I've eaten at along the trail, this was the only one where I ever got such a feeling. I ate my meal and moved on.

I crossed the Umatilla at Pendleton but rather than climbing back up on the bluffs, I followed the river downstream on Reith Road. The road trended downhill, but there were enough small climbs to keep me from coasting all the way to Echo.

Five miles before Echo, I came to the marker for Corral Springs. This was where the trail dropped from the bluffs back to the river's edge. Supposedly there are some nice swales about a quarter mile beyond the marker but the land is private and I didn't want to trespass. I later learned that the landowner does allow people to walk to the ruts but that knowledge didn't help me at the time.

At the south edge of Echo lies the grave of pioneer David Koontz. It's enclosed in a small wooden fence and an OCTA sign tells his story. He was born in Ohio in 1830. In 1852, he headed west with a train of 24 wagons. Everyone in his train was related. He died that year at the age of 22 but there is no record of exactly when or how he died. The Boy Scouts found his grave in 1915 and built the fence around it. A wooden sign nailed to the fence serves as his headstone. At Fort Henrietta Park in Echo, the town maintains a small RV park and campground. It's well kept but of the four RVs parked there, three appeared permanent. I pitched the only tent that night.

The actual Fort Henrietta was built on the west bank of the Umatilla River but the park is on the east side. The Whitman Massacre of 1847 (in which Marcus Whitman, his wife Narcissa, and 12 other whites were murdered) sparked several years of fighting known as the

Cayuse War. In the aftermath of the war, the Umatilla (sometimes called Utilla) Agency House was built in 1851. It was situated next to the Oregon Trail just beyond the Umatilla River crossing (the Lower Crossing). This was the first wood-framed building the emigrants saw since Wyoming. In November 1855, the house was burned to the ground at the start of the Yakima War.   Almost immediately, a detachment of the First Oregon Mounted Rifles arrived at the site and constructed Fort Henrietta. It was 100 feet square with two bastions located at opposite corners. A replica blockhouse in Fort Henrietta Park represents one of these bastions. As for the actual fort, it was abandoned in 1856.

      After pitching my tent and getting cleaned up, I walked into downtown Echo for dinner. It wasn't a long walk. The whole downtown consists of only two blocks. My mealtime choices were sparse. There was a brew house that wasn't open, a winery, or the H&P Café. I opted for the café and was glad I did. Their pulled pork sandwich was one of the best I've ever had.

Sunday, September 4ᵗʰ - Echo, OR, to Cecil, OR - 49 miles

      From Echo, I crossed the Umatilla River and headed west along Oregon Trail Road. Right before reaching Highway 207 I passed a brown BLM sign directing visitors to a protected area called Echo Meadows. From the pioneers' standpoint there was nothing significant about the site. Its importance lies in the fact that it inspired the creation of the modern Oregon – California Trails Association. According to historian Tom Laidlaw, when author Gregory Franzwa first visited the area in 1971, several miles of pristine trail ruts were visible. When he returned to the site ten years later, Franzwa discovered most of the ruts had been plowed over. He decided to bring together a group of like-minded friends and, in 1982, OCTA was formed. I didn't take time to leave the pavement and visit these ruts; they are located at the end of a half-mile gravel road. It's nice to know, however, that someone cared enough to preserve them.

      I turned south on Highway 207 but the trail continued more westerly towards Butter Creek. As far as water sources go, Butter Creek wasn't much. It was, unfortunately, the only water there would be for another 15 miles. My route along Highway 207 followed Butter Creek upstream for six miles before turning west and making a crossing. After the bridge I started a short but steep climb to the bluffs west of

The Cecil Store is all that remains of the historic community of Cecil, Oregon. *45.618358, -119.959728*

Preparing to ford the John Day River at McDonald, Oregon. *45.589439, -120.409045*

the creek.

My slight detour south from the trail was necessary for two reasons. First, there are no roads, paved or unpaved, that follow the trail across the private lands in this area. Secondly, as the trail continues westward it eventually enters the US Navy's Boardman Bombing Range. It's still an active military training area, so access is limited. Permission to cross the area can often be obtained so long as it doesn't interfere with ongoing operations. I zigzagged around the countryside for a while, staying as close as practical to the trail. I finally turned west onto Immigrant Lane (note the County's use of the wrong word). This road runs along the southern boundary of the bombing range and passes by Well Springs.

Pioneers described Well Springs as little better than a mud hole. Sometimes it was necessary to fill a cloth bag with mud and squeeze out the water to drink. This is part of the reason why Butter Creek was so important to the travelers. Depending on Well Springs wasn't always a wise thing to do. Beyond this point the next source of water was Willow Creek, another 15 miles up the trail.

The mud flats of Well Springs straddle Immigrant Lane. On the south side, a kiosk with interpretive panels has been built. The shade it provided turned out to be a good place for a picnic. On the north side of the road, the Navy has cleared an area of any surprises and opened it up for public access. A number of signboards have also been placed within this area to explain not only the history but also the ecology of the landscape. Even today it's bleak country.

A half mile west of Well Springs is a pioneer cemetery. Only two graves have been identified: Robert Williams and Dorothy Kane. Williams died in 1852 but Kane's year of death is unknown. In the 1920s, 13 graves were marked. All those markers have since crumbled to dust. No one knows how many folks are actually buried in or near this plot of land. There is also a memorial for Colonel Cornelius Gilliam. He was in charge of the Oregon volunteer militia during the Cayuse War. Near this site on March 24, 1848, he was killed when his gun got tangled in some rope and accidentally fired. He was initially buried here, but later he was reinterred near his home in the Willamette Valley.

Another 15 miles brought me to Willow Creek and the Krebs Ranch. The Oregon Trail crossed the creek just downstream from the main ranch house. In the late 1800s, a general store with a post office was established here. It became the "town" of Cecil.

As I was planning my route through this area, I contacted the landowners and asked for permission to camp next to Willow Creek. They said they could do even better. They would leave the door to the Cecil Store, which still occupies its original site, open for me. I was welcomed to sleep inside. I was planning to sleep on the floor but a few weeks before starting this year's ride the landowners told me the back side of the store had been converted to a hunting lodge. There were bunk beds, a bathroom and shower, and a kitchen inside. I was free to make myself at home. Unfortunately, being the Labor Day weekend, they added that no one would be around. Although I didn't get a chance to meet them, I greatly appreciated their hospitality.

Monday, September 5th - Cecil, OR, to Wasco, OR - 45 miles

Of my entire journey along the Oregon Trail, this was perhaps my most difficult day. It wasn't the distance that made it so challenging: it was the terrain and wind. I left Cecil at 7:30 a.m., but I didn't roll into Wasco until almost 8:30 p.m.

Departing Cecil, I immediately had a 500 foot climb out of the Willow Creek valley. Once on the plateau, all I could see were wind turbines in every direction. I read somewhere this was the second largest windfarm in the world. Luckily they hadn't woken up yet. They were barely spinning at all.

As I descended down the western slope of this plateau, I entered Four Mile Canyon. I soon came to a nice little BLM kiosk where the trail crossed the roadway. Ruts were plainly visible on the hill west of the kiosk. I continued on another two and a half miles until I came to Eightmile Canyon Road. At the intersection I turned back to the southwest and started up the canyon. After a mile the route turned west again and I had to go up and over another high ridge. When I got back down to the base of this ridge I started a gradual descent into the valley of the John Day River.

My whole timetable for the 2016 leg of this journey was based on crossing the John Day River. The Oregon Trail crossed the John Day at what came to be called McDonald's Ford or McDonalds's Ferry. Now the spot is just called McDonald on the map. No bridge was ever built there. If I was going to cross at McDonald, I had to time it to when the flow of the river was at its lowest. The US Geological Survey (USGS) maintains an automated flowmeter at McDonald and the information is available online. I reviewed the previous ten years of data and concluded that the "normal" low flow occurs during the first two weeks of September. In the springtime the flow can exceed 5,000 cubic feet per second (cfs). In early September, however, the flow is typically less than 100 cfs. I contacted the scientists at the BLM office in Prineville, Oregon, and was told I could safely walk across the river so long as the flow was below 400 cfs. As soon as I could get a cell signal after leaving Cecil, I checked the USGS website. The John Day's flow rate was 24 cfs. I was good to go.

When I arrived at the John Day River I was momentarily confused by a BLM sign. The sign directed all boaters to the left. I knew the ford was to the right but for some reason I followed the sign to the left. After a few hundred yards, however, I came to my senses and turned around. Back on track, I followed a gravel road for a mile. On the right side of the road was an old stone "Oregon Trail" marker that was almost hidden in the weeds. To the left, the road approached the ford.

I parked my bike at the water's edge and dug deep down into my panniers for the sandals I had packed specifically for this occasion. I didn't want to get my shoes wet, and the rocks would have made a barefoot crossing tricky. I removed the panniers from the trailer and carried them one at a time across the river. It was 100 yards wide, but the water never came higher than my shins. The flow was almost unnoticeable. Algae on the rocks, though, forced me to consider each step carefully. With the bags safely on the other side, I made one last crossing with my bike and trailer.

The pioneers usually reached the John Day in early to mid-October. The water would have been a bit higher and faster but, in most years, not by much. This was probably one of their easier river crossings of the trip. The next climb, though, was not so easy.

Remember that the prairie schooners of the day had a very, very large turning radius. They were not capable of doing switchbacks. Also remember that they were top heavy. This made them prone to tipping over sideways. Any hill the emigrants encountered had to be met straight up or straight down. The climb up from the John Day River was 700 feet in two thirds of a mile. That calculates to a 20% grade! It just amazes me that they found the strength to do that.

My climb out of the valley was difficult enough. At least I had a road. Following this gravel road up a tributary's canyon, I gained over 800 feet in almost two miles. That's an 8% grade. I was whipped as I approached the top of the canyon.

There is no marker at the top of the canyon but near this point a seldom used shortcut began. The main trail turned northwest towards The Dalles. The shortcut headed southwest towards Tygh Valley and the Barlow Road. It wasn't necessarily a bad shortcut. The majority of the wagons, however, continued to The Dalles. At this point on their journey most travelers would have been low on provisions. Whether their plan was to follow the Barlow Road or float down the Columbia River, the Dalles offered them a chance to re-supply. Also, I suspect, more than a few pioneers went to the The Dalles just for the opportunity to glimpse some semblance of civilization. In 1860, a bridge was built across the Deschutes River at Sherars Falls on the shortcut. As a result, more wagons began using this route and bypassing The Dalles altogether.

Now that I was on top of a plateau again, the winds hit me full force. And, of course, they were headwinds. I was surrounded by rapidly spinning wind turbines. It was only 12 more miles to Wasco, but it took me over three hours to get there. I had reservations at the Wasco House Bed and Breakfast for the evening. Since it was already after 5:00 p.m., I called to let the owners know I still planned to spend

Looking down from Old Moody Road into the area of Celilo, Oregon.
45.641229, -120.982427

the night there. I told them I expected to arrive around 7:00 p.m. When I did get there, it was almost 8:30 p.m. Dave, one of the owners, had actually driven out onto the highway to look for me. He pulled up behind me as I parked my bike. My first question to him was if he had a vacancy for the next night. If ever I deserved a rest day, the following day would be it. I also asked him if there was a café or store in town. He said everything was closed for Labor Day. Dave then offered to drive me to Biggs Junction so I could get something to eat. It was an offer I couldn't refuse.

Tuesday, September 6ᵗʰ - Rest Day in Wasco, OR - 0 miles

After the previous day's long ordeal I decided a rest day was in order. I booked another night at the Wasco House Bed and Breakfast. The owners, Dave and Lisa, both enjoy cycling so they understand our special needs. Dave gave me some advice on the safest and easiest route from Wasco to the Columbia River. I was planning to take Highway 97 but he said the large number of trucks that use that route makes it unsafe for cyclists. He recommended Highway 206 instead. There are a couple of climbs at the beginning but then it's downhill all the way to the river. It sounded like my kind of route.

Following a delicious breakfast, Lisa told me she had to go feed her chickens down the road. She asked if I wanted to walk along. I told her I've noticed that raising chickens for fresh eggs seems to be really popular these days. She said in Portland a lot of people are doing it now. In Louisiana, even our Governor has chicken coops behind his official residence in Baton Rouge. Later, Lisa had to deliver some apples to the community center in Moro. It's a few miles down the road from Wasco and she asked if I wanted to ride with her. She suggested I visit the Moro history museum while she delivered the apples. For such a small town, Moro had a really impressive museum. I'm glad I checked it out.

All in all it was a very relaxing day. I reviewed my route from The Dalles to Rock Creek Reservoir. I had planned to ride the fifty miles in one day but, when I looked at the elevation profile, I realized it would involve roughly 5,000 feet of climbing. I could probably do it but since I didn't see the point of killing myself I decided to break that day into two. In my opinion, if touring by bicycle ever stops being fun, there's no reason to do it.

Wednesday, September 7th - Wasco, OR, to The Dalles, OR - 32 miles

Well rested and well fed, I left Wasco in much better condition than when I arrived. Based on Dave's suggestion, I followed Highway 206 out of town. A few miles down the road I saw an old church next to the highway. From a distance I thought there was hay stacked inside, but as I got closer I saw it was empty. The church was the Locust Grove Methodist Church but I couldn't tell if it was being renovated or demolished. I just thought it looked interesting.

By taking Highway 206 I hit the Columbia River a couple of miles west of where the emigrants would have first seen it. Their trail would have put them at the river just west of present day Biggs Junction. If I had followed Highway 97 instead, I would have been closer to the original trail. The price, though, would have been a more dangerous ride. Highway 206 was definitely the better choice.

At the Columbia River the emigrants and I turned downriver and followed it to the mouth of the Deschutes River. In pioneer days this was a difficult crossing. Depending on the water levels when they arrived, sandbars could sometimes be used as stepping stones to cross the river. If the water was too high, Indians were often hired to guide the wagons across. Today, with all the dams on the Columbia, the water levels of both rivers are much deeper. Thankfully, I had the advantage of a bridge.

As I crossed the Deschutes I was amazed by the number of trucks and boat trailers parked beside the road. I stopped on the bridge and talked to a couple of fishermen. I asked them what they were fishing for and they said they would be happy to catch anything on that day. Nothing was biting. Next I asked them about the bait they were using. They said they had to use artificial lures when they were in the Deschutes, but if they went out into the Columbia's waters they could use live bait. As I understand it, the restriction was put into place to prevent overfishing on the Deschutes and its tributaries.

On the west side of the Deschutes I stopped into a small park to refill my water bottles and take a break. I saw an Oregon Fish and Wildlife agent questioning boaters when they docked. I asked her if she was conducting boater safety inspections like our agents often do. Instead, she was surveying their catches. She added that the steelhead and salmon catches had been dismal recently.

The Historic Balch Hotel in Dufur, Oregon. *45.450449, -121.131646*

Leaving the Deschutes behind, I started a short but steep climb up Old Moody Road. It wasn't as difficult as I expected, and when I got to the top I was rewarded with some spectacular views of the Columbia River. I almost felt sorry for those poor souls locked in their cars driving along the Interstate. Such is the price for speed.

The emigrants also had to climb this bluff. The cliffs move in so close to the river here that wagons could not continue along the south bank. They didn't follow the exact route I was on but surely they must have been impressed by similar views.

As I was riding along the top of the bluff I was able to look down onto Celilo. For 15,000 years native tribes had lived in villages at the site. In fact, until 1957, it was the longest continually inhabited community on the North American continent. The Indians fished from platforms built out over a series of rapids and cascades on the river. This tradition and way of life came to an abrupt end with the completion of The Dalles Dam in 1957. All of the cascades were submerged under the rising waters of the Columbia.

After five miles on the high ground I finally started my descent into The Dalles. For some purists The Dalles was the end of the Oregon Trail. Until the Barlow Road opened in 1846, all wagon traffic

173

stopped here. The wagons were dismantled and loaded, along with the families and their possessions, onto rafts. Most of the rafts were then launched into the Columbia River from the mouth of Chenoweth Creek (now overlooked by a huge Google Data Center). While they floated dangerously down the Columbia, their livestock was driven over one of the two established cattle trails to the Willamette Valley.

The name "The Dalles" meant something entirely different during emigration days. Today it refers to the city but to the pioneers it referred to two sets of swift and treacherous rapids that once existed ten miles upriver from the present city. In 1843, if you recall, the Applegates set out on boats from the confluence of the Walla Walla and Columbia Rivers. When they entered the rapids one of their boats capsized. Brothers Jesse and Lindsay Applegate both lost young sons to The Dalles. This tragedy motivated them, along with Levi Scott, to find a safer route into the Willamette Valley from the south. In 1846, the first wagons followed the Southern Route from Fort Hall. This route is now commonly called "The Applegate Trail".

I had initially wanted to take a rest day in The Dalles but since I had just taken one in Wasco, I decided to limit my stay to one night. I didn't see much of the town but what I did experience was a lot of traffic and congestion. The downtown, close to the river, was not very bike friendly. At lunch I stopped at a brew house on 2nd Street (the main drag) and locked my bike to a light pole in front of the building. Before I got inside one of the waiters came out and said I would have to park the bike around back. Neither the city nor any businesses I saw provided bicycle racks. Apparently, though, the city will ticket anyone who dares to lock a bike to a light pole. It wasn't a problem moving my bike to the rear of the building, I just get nervous when I can't see it from where I'm sitting. Bicycle theft is one of the greatest fears of touring cyclists. After lunch I stopped into a local bike shop to pick up some new brake shoes. With all the hills I'd already crossed, my brakes were going soft. I knew I had plenty of braking left to do on this ride.

Thursday, September 8th - The Dalles, OR, to Dufur, OR - 16 miles

· When I made the decision to split the ride from The Dalles to Rock Creek Reservoir into two days, I had to choose between Dufur and Tygh Valley as my overnight stops. Both towns had campgrounds but the one in Dufur didn't have good online reviews. On the other hand, Dufur had an old historic hotel that looked promising. The more I read about the Balch Hotel, the more I wanted to spend a night there. So Dufur it was.

There were three big but gradual climbs on the road from The Dalles to Dufur. Between them were three major creeks. The pioneers were never especially imaginative when naming bodies of water. I can't tell you how many Willow Creeks and Rock Creeks I'd crossed since Missouri. When they turned south from The Dalles, however, it's like they didn't even try to come up with good names anymore. In order of crossing, the creeks were Threemile Creek, Fivemile Creek, and Eightmile Creek. The names reflected their distances from The Dalles. Following my final descent into Dufur, I smiled when I learned the town was situated on the banks of Fifteenmile Creek.

It was noon when I arrived in Dufur. I went straight to the Balch Hotel. Normal check-in time at the Balch is 4:00 p.m., but being a Thursday, I was fairly confident a room would be clean and available. It was. As I was talking to the desk clerk I asked her for some lunch and dinner recommendations. She said Kramer's Store had a great deli and the Pastime Saloon was good for dinner. She added that the Pastime would be full of "colorful characters and had lots of dead animals on

Tygh Valley, Oregon, facing west towards Mt. Hood. *45.246395, -121.179162*

the wall." She turned out to be right on all accounts.

Even though the Balch Hotel wasn't around in the Oregon Trail years (neither was Dufur for that matter), it is steeped in history. It opened for business in 1908. In the decades that followed, it was a hotel, a boarding house, and a private residence. In recent years it was restored to its former glory and reopened for visitors. Like the original, the current hotel has a lobby, a parlor, and a dining room on the first floor. Guest rooms are on the second and third floors. Most rooms share a bathroom at the end of the hallway, but a couple of third floor rooms have their own private baths (a concession to less adventurous modern guests). I opted for a traditional room.

After cleaning up, I walked down to Kramer's Store for lunch. While I was sitting inside eating a sandwich I noticed the ceiling fans. Unlike modern fans with individual motors, these fans were all connected by belts to a single motor. This caught my attention because in one of my favorite John Wayne movies, *The Shootist*, the final gunfight takes place in a saloon called the Metropole. The Metropole had the same type of ceiling fans. Sometimes the smallest things catch my eye.

From Kramer's I walked up to the U.S. Forest Service's district office. I had some questions about Forest Road 3530 in the Hood National Forest. The last ten miles of this road lies directly on top of the original Barlow Road. I wanted to ride that stretch but the Forest Service's website said numerous downed trees were blocking the road. The website, however, had not been updated since May. The ranger assured me the road had been cleared for travel. That's what I needed to hear. I also asked her about black bears in the area. She said that they shouldn't be a concern. During her 24 years with the Forest Service she had only ever seen two.

As I said before, some people consider The Dalles to be the end of the Oregon Trail. When the Barlow Road opened in 1846, however, wagons could continue past The Dalles to their ultimate destination: Oregon City. Oregon City, at the time, was the seat of government in the area. No matter where the emigrants eventually settled, they had to go to Oregon City to file their land claims.

Sam Barlow was the leader of one of six (some say seven) wagon trains that left Missouri in 1845. Not long into the migration all of the trains became intermingled. On any given day it was impossible to tell which, or how many, wagons belonged to a specific train. When Barlow's group arrived at The Dalles in September, he was appalled at the long wait required until boats would be available to carry everyone down the Columbia. He set out with seven wagons to find a better way around Mt. Hood. The route I followed was very close to Barlow's route. By 1845, a wagon road already existed between The Dalles and Tygh Valley, so technically Barlow's trail blazing didn't start until he turned west from the existing road. This old road came right through the middle of Dufur but, as I said, the town didn't exist at the time.

Friday, September 9th - Dufur, OR, to Rock Creek Reservoir, OR - 29 miles

When I left the Balch Hotel in the morning none of the staff was up and moving around yet. I put the key (a real key, not a card) into the slot on the wall behind the desk for Room 5. I stopped off at Kramer's one more time for a honeybun and some chocolate milk. As I was leaving Dufur, I passed the town's RV park. It didn't look as bad as some of the online reviews said. Actually, it didn't look bad at all. Still, I didn't regret staying at the Balch. It's always nice when someone invests their time and resources to preserve a bit of the past. From Dufur it was a slow, gradual climb. At the twelve mile mark I reached the top of Tygh Ridge. A quick five mile descent through Butler Canyon into Tygh Valley was my reward.

In 1845, soon after Sam Barlow headed south, Joel Palmer arrived at The Dalles. It's not clear whether Barlow and Palmer knew each other already. Given the fluid nature of the 1845 migration, though, they most certainly had heard of each other. Both men were prudent leaders. Neither had taken the Greenwood – Sublette Cutoff in Wyoming and neither had been tempted to follow Stephen Meek on his "shortcut" up the Malheur River in eastern Oregon. When Palmer learned that Barlow was looking for a wagon route around Mt. Hood, however, he decided to follow with 23 wagons of his own. He caught up with Barlow's seven wagons at Tygh Valley.

It was almost time for lunch when I came into Tygh Valley. For some reason, I thought that Dufur was the smaller of the two towns. I was wrong. I stopped at the post office and asked if there was a restaurant nearby. Only one, I was told. So off I went to find Molly B's Diner. A young waitress greeted me. She looked not much older than high school aged. I asked her if I was too early for lunch. She peeked at the clock on the wall and replied, "Yep, you gotta wait 20 minutes. I can take your order now, but she won't start cooking it until 11:00." Now I can see some corporate restaurant chain being inflexible on

Forest Road 3530 was built directly on the remnants of the original Barlow Road, east of Barlow Pass, Oregon. *45.226486, -121.620326*

such trivialities, but a local diner. Really? So I just ordered an omelet and that was that. I guess when you're the only game in town you get to call the shots. I was later told I made a big mistake by not ordering one of Molly B's cinnamon rolls.

The climb out of Tygh Valley was steep for the wagon trains. It was just as high for me but the modern road lessened the grade.

I was up on the plateau with minimal effort. Once at the top, it was relatively flat the rest of the way to Rock Creek Reservoir. At Wamic I continued due west, whereas the original Barlow Road angled slightly to the south. By the time I arrived at Rock Creek Reservoir, a gap of roughly two and a half miles separated our routes.

My road out of Wamic was good until I crossed into the Hood National Forest. Normally roads within National Forests and National Parks are better than the surrounding local roads. That was not the case here. Forest Road 48 had an unusual pattern of cracking I'd never seen before. Every 30 yards or so, a crack in the asphalt stretched all the way across the road. Most of the cracks were six to eight inches wide and one or two inches deep. In a car these cracks would cause an annoying thump-thump-thump sound. On a bicycle they presented a bigger challenge. Each crack was a little different so each one had to be studied and crossed at the best spot. Hitting any of them wrong could have resulted in a broken spoke or bent wheel. Fortunately I wasn't in a hurry so I didn't have any problems.

I looked at the bad pavement as more than a mere sign of poor maintenance. In a broader sense, to me it represented a larger problem

Pioneer Woman's Grave, located near the intersection of the old Barlow Road and the old Highway 35 at Barlow Pass, Oregon. *45.281922, -121.700320*

our society faces today. The original roadbed was probably made of concrete. As this foundation eroded, layer upon layer of asphalt was applied as quick fixes. The underlying cause was never addressed. As the foundation continues to shift, cracks reappear on the thin surface. Likewise, as the foundation of our country's infrastructure crumbles around us, superficial solutions are all we can seem to manage.

When I arrived at the Forest Service campground at Rock Creek Reservoir I asked the camp host if the pavement along Forest Road 48 eventually improved. She thought about it for a second and then replied that it got better in eight miles. Great. I also noticed there was little water in the reservoir. She said the lake fills in the springtime but it is used for irrigation throughout the summer.

Saturday, September 10ᵗʰ - Rock Creek Reservoir, OR, to Still Creek, OR - 28 miles

Heading south from Rock Creek Reservoir, I began to close the gap between my location and the old Barlow Road. When Forest Road 48 made its turn from south to west, I was within a mile of Barlow's original route. As I continued west both roads angled closer together.

Soon after making the turn I came to the small bridge across Gate Creek. A half mile downstream from this bridge Barlow, constructed his first tollgate. Through the years a total of five tollgates were used but only one at any given time. Their location was based on where the toll collector lived; usually the gate was near the keeper's home. This first tollgate operated from 1846 through 1852.

For the first four miles after leaving my campsite, I had to deal with those cracks across the pavement. Luckily my host was wrong about the distance before the pavement improved. My ride became peaceful when the cracks disappeared. One of the great pleasures of traveling by bicycle is when the road is smooth and the bike is well tuned there is almost no noise. Even the faintest sounds of the countryside or forest can be appreciated. The only potential problem is that you can surprise someone or something unintentionally. I was silently gliding along this road when, all of a sudden, I heard a loud noise in the brush to my right. It was something like a cross between a snort and a bark. Was it a bear? Was it an elk? Maybe it was a raccoon with a sinus infection. I don't know. I never saw anything but I quickened my pace nonetheless. Once I had put some distance between myself and the phantom sound, I stopped and retrieved the bear spray from my panniers. I had bought this can in Wyoming two years earlier. It still had the safety tie on the trigger. I removed the tie and put the spray in one of my water bottle cages. It was now within easy reach should a need arise. It didn't, of course.

The Barlow Road crossed from the east side of the White River to the west side a mile before the bridge on Forest Road 43. I turned onto this road and crossed the bridge. The pioneers named it the White River because high levels of glacial silt gave the water a milky white appearance. It still does. A short distance beyond the bridge Forest Road 43 crosses Forest Road 3530, the Barlow Road. At this intersection is a sign that describes Fort Deposit.

In 1845, as Barlow and Palmer and their followers inched their way up the eastern slope of Mt. Hood, it became clear to all involved that winter was not far off. Each day crews had been cutting a wagon road up the mountain while scouts ventured ahead to mark the trail. On one of these scouting expeditions, Palmer ascended high onto a glacier and observed what he believed to be the Willamette Valley. He knew he had found the route but he also knew following it would not be easy. In mid-October the group decided to cache their wagons and possessions at a site they dubbed Fort Deposit. One person would be left behind to guard the cache while everyone else would continue to the Willamette on foot or horseback.

The actual location of Fort Deposit remains controversial. For years it was believed to be in a clearing a mile below Barlow Pass called the Devil's Half Acre. Later, historians decided it was more likely located near the confluence of Barlow Creek and the White River. This is where the interpretive sign stands today. Now the general consensus is that Fort Deposit was located in an area known as Klinger's Camp, roughly half way between the two previous sites. The bottom line is nobody really knows.

Aside from the question of Fort Deposit's location, the next big question is how the Barlow – Palmer party made it through to the Willamette Valley. Some historians believe the livestock and the people continued on along the route seen by Palmer. This is the path that would eventually become the Barlow Road. Considering the cautious nature of both Barlow and Palmer, however, I doubt they would have allowed the women and children to continue on a yet unproven route with winter approaching. There is some evidence that from Fort Deposit the livestock was driven by a few men along the future road. These

Summit Meadows with Mt. Hood in the background, near Government Camp, Oregon. *45.283953, -121.736696*

men were tasked to mark the trail as they moved down the mountain. The rest of the people, the families, turned northward and followed a network of Indian trails until they intersected the established cattle trail that connected The Dalles to the Willamette Valley. And finally, other historians believe that only four men continued directly to the Willamette, again marking the trail as they went along. Everyone else, along with the livestock, returned to The Dalles by the route they had just cleared. From The Dalles some followed the cattle trail and some took boats.

The problem with answering both where and how questions is that no physical evidence has been found. All that historians have to go on are written accounts recorded years after the fact. It is almost impossible to tease the truth from the embellishment. And, as any criminologist knows, eyewitness accounts are the least reliable form of evidence. To paraphrase an ancient Taoist proverb: Those who know the truth can't reveal it, and those that proclaim the truth can't know it. Regardless of the specifics, the wagons were cached, a guard was left behind, the eventual route was blazed, and everyone made it safely to Oregon City by early November.

I rode past the Fort Deposit sign and onto Forest Road

3530. For the next seven miles, this road lies directly on or beside the original Barlow Road. Initially the road was smooth but sandy. Almost immediately I crossed Barlow Creek. From that point on I followed the creek up to its head. Three miles into this stretch brought me to Klinger's Camp (one of the possible Fort Deposit sites). Beyond there the road began to get much rockier. Along the way I also noticed wooden posts with "Oregon Trail" markings. These cedar posts were placed along the Barlow Road by the Forest Service as part of a Bicentennial project. The placement of the posts was random, but so long as I saw one from time to time I knew I was on the right path.

The further I rode, the rockier the road became. I actually had a couple of mountain bikers and motorcyclists approach me from the opposite direction. My touring bike, however, just wasn't designed for this rough of a trail. I finally decided it was a nice day for a hike. For the last couple of miles up to Barlow Pass, I traveled the same way most of the emigrants traveled. I walked.

At the crest of Barlow Pass, Forest Road 3530 connects to a piece of the old Highway 35. This highway, incidentally, was one segment of the Mt. Hood Loop Highway which opened in 1925. I turned southwest onto this road and a half mile later stopped at an overlook to gaze upon Mt. Hood. On the opposite side of the road I noticed a spring that had been built up to resemble a water fountain. I later learned this was one of the so-called "radiator springs" that were built in the 1920s so drivers could add water to their overheating car engines as they came up the mountain. Another mile and a half brought me to the Pioneer Woman's Grave. I'd visited a lot of pioneer graves along the trail but this one was perhaps the saddest. Imagine the lady walking 2,000 miles across dusty trails, successfully crossing the last major pass, only to die within sight of the promise land. And nobody even remembers her name. The grave was found in 1924 by workers while constructing the Mt. Hood Highway. It has since become a minor shrine.

My peaceful ride down the old highway came to an end when I reached the modern multilane Highway 35. It got even worse when I joined U.S. Highway 26. Traffic on this road was heavy and fast. It wasn't much different than an Interstate. Ongoing construction, though, had reduced the shoulder to gravel. I had two miles of this insanity before I turned onto Perry Vickers Road and entered the Forest Service campground at Still Creek.

A sign at the campground's entrance stated "Campground Full,

A replica of the fifth and final Barlow Road Tollgate, near Rhododendron, Oregon. *45.319759, -121.903435*

No Vacancy." I tracked down the host, Tom, and asked him if there wasn't some little patch of grass where a poor bicycle traveler might pitch his tent for the night. As luck would have it, Tom had done some bicycle touring in his younger days. He was sympathetic to my plight and showed me a place behind the picnic area where I could camp. The site turned out to be atop the foundation of the old post office and general store for the resort of Swim, Oregon. The resort was first developed around 1915 to take advantage of a small hot spring located nearby. A concrete pool was built, hence the name. The post office served the area until 1929. The Barlow Road passed within 100 yards of the building.

Later that evening as I was talking with Tom about my trip, I mentioned I wanted to stay another night at Still Creek before riding on. I supposed that the next day being a Sunday, there would be some vacant campsites available. He replied there would be plenty of empty campsites because this was the last night the Forest Service campgrounds would be open. Everything was scheduled to be locked up on Sunday afternoon until the next year.

Sunday, September 11th, Rest Day at Government Camp, OR – 4 miles

I had planned this to be a rest day and I had expected to spend it resting at the Still Creek campground. The Forest Service, however, had other plans. They decided that the 2016 camping season was now over. All of the campgrounds in this Ranger District were to be closed later in the day.

I slept in late for a change. For the first time in a long while, I woke up to a damp tent. My clothes were damp, my sleeping bag was damp, and I was damp. It was also cold, about 41°F at daybreak. I stayed under the covers as long as I could.

Eventually I got packed up and I rode south out of the campground on Perry Vickers Road. The road leads to Summit Meadows, a favorite pioneer campground. There is a small cemetery containing three graves next to the clearing. One grave belongs to Mr. Vickers. He was the toll collector at the third of the Barlow Road's tollgates. The gate was located next to Vickers' home at Summit

The Sandy River, looking downstream from the present Revenue Bridge, at Sandy, Oregon. The original Revenue Bridge and the 2nd Barlow Road Tollgate were located near the river's last visible bend in the photograph. *45.407721, -122.235039*

Meadows and operated from 1866 to 1871. Perry Vickers lost his life in 1883 when, as a member of a posse, the horse thief he was pursuing got the jump on him.

On one side of Vickers' grave is an illegible marker. No one knows who is buried there. On the other side of Perry is the grave of Baby Barclay. He was the two-month-old son of a family visiting Summit Meadows in 1882. Fifty yards north of the cemetery is another grave that is easily overlooked. This is the final resting place of Baby Morgan. She was born in June, 1847 near Independence Rock, Wyoming. Her mother died soon after the child's birth and is interred at the landmark. The baby girl was cared for by family and friends until they reached Summit Meadows. Here, some sort of accident reunited the child with her mother.

Following my visit to Summit Meadows, I rode back through the Still Creek campground. I continued a few miles up the road to the town of Government Camp. While eating lunch I noticed a laundromat next to the restaurant so I took time to wash some clothes before riding on to my hotel. Government Camp is a very hectic place. During the winter it's a haven for skiers. The historic Timberline Lodge is a short distance away. Another resort, Ski Bowl, operates as an adventure park during the summer months. On this day, over 7,000 tourists squeezed into Government Camp to visit the resorts. I was glad they weren't planning to spend the night.

Next to my hotel was the Mt. Hood Brewing Company. The beer was good. The pizza was good. What really caught my attention, though, were the menus. Besides having the main menu and a kids menu, they had a Dog Menu "just for your canine friend." Where else can a person order Frozen Yogurt Peanut Butter Balls for their dog? Only in Oregon!

Monday, September 12ᵗʰ - Government Camp, OR, to Barton Park, OR - 42 miles

There are days when every bicycle tourist asks themselves if it's all really worth it. This was NOT one of those days. It was the type of day we dream about. Mostly downhill. A slight tailwind. Cool but not cold. Beautiful scenery. Before I tell you about my ride, however, let me give you some more Barlow Road history.

Over the winter of 1845/46, Sam Barlow requested and received a charter from Oregon's provisional government to build and operate a toll road. Officially called the Mt. Hood Road, it almost immediately became known as the Barlow Road. With financial backing from Philip Foster, Barlow prepared to return to the mountains in the spring. Joel Palmer, however, stepped away from the roadbuilding project. He returned to Illinois, only to lead another wagon train west the following year.

When the winter snows had melted sufficiently, a team of 40 men worked their way back up the west side of Mt. Hood. There is some question as to whether Sam Barlow was with this crew, but probably his son William was. Following marks left on trees the previous autumn, the men cleared the path of anything that could be cut down or moved and went around those obstacles that wouldn't budge. They didn't do any dirt work. Gullies and ridges remained unaltered. They finally reached the point where the roadbuilding ended months before: Barlow Pass. The wagons and possessions cached at Fort Deposit were retrieved, and the Barlow Road was opened for business.

As a toll road, the Barlow Road operated from 1846 to 1918. Barlow himself lost interest within a couple of years and it was never a money maker for any of the subsequent operators. Though it was the last link in the long overland trail from Missouri, by 1860 emigrant traffic had begun to wane. Travel on the Columbia River became easier and cheaper in the late 1850s. Larger boats and better pilots plied the waters and wooden rail lines (with mules pulling the cars) made the portages faster. The Barlow Road remained the favored choice, however, for emigrants traveling with large herds of livestock. Tolls were still collected on the road until 1918. In 1919 the historic route was donated to the State of Oregon.

When I left the hotel I was worried about riding on US Highway 26. My experience from a couple days earlier was not pleasant. On this day, however, the road construction worked in my favor. One of the two downhill lanes had recently been resurfaced but was yet to be striped. Barricades kept the cars on the inside lane and I had the outside lane to myself for many miles.

I soon found myself on Laurel Hill. It's not really a hill. According to historian Dr. Jim Tompkins, it's actually a pluton (I had to look up the definition, too.) Mt. Hood is a volcano. Eons ago a subsurface flow of magma created this peninsula-like feature the pioneers named Laurel Hill. It was easy to get on but a royal pain to get off of. Through the years of trail travel five separate "chutes" developed. As one chute eroded to the point of no longer being useable the road just shifted over to the next available spot. The chutes were basically very, very steep grades where the wagons skidded down the side of Laurel Hill.

Chute #3 is the most accessible of the five chutes today. A short hiking trail leads you from US Highway 26, first to the middle of the chute and then around to the top. I didn't walk to the top, however. I was paranoid about leaving my bicycle unattended for too long by the side of the highway.

Further down the road, right before the town of Rhododendron, I came to where the fifth and final Barlow Road tollgate was located. It operated from 1883 to 1918. A replica of that tollgate exists there today. The large maple trees on either side of the gate were planted by the last gatekeeper.

I had intended to turn off US Highway 26 and jog north on Lolo Pass Road to Barlow Trail Road. This was the route of the original road. When I got to Lolo Pass Road, however, there was a flashing construction sign that proclaimed, "Barlow Trail Road closed one mile west of Lolo Pass Road." The Zigzag Ranger Station is located at that intersection so I went inside to get more information. All they could tell me was Barlow Trail Road was closed in the middle section. That meant nothing to me. I decided to follow the detour signs and hope for the best.

Five more miles along US Highway 26 brought me to the Brightwood Loop, onto which the detour signs directed me. Soon thereafter, I crossed a bridge over the Sandy River and connected with Barlow Trail Road. No harm done.

Barlow Trail Road eventually turns into East Marmot Road. Beyond that, a climb of 500 feet got me to the top of a ridge the emigrants called the Devil's Backbone. Riding along this ridge was great. It felt like I was riding on a country road somewhere in New England on a pleasant autumn day. Farm houses and pastures dotted the landscape. Even though the top of the Devil's Backbone was relatively level, the nearby valley of the Sandy River continued to fall to the west. Coming off the ridge and back to the Sandy, I lost nearly 1,000 feet of elevation.

I crossed the Sandy River on a modern bridge called the Revenue Bridge. It takes its name from a historic bridge that once stood nearby. In the 1850s, Francis Revenue established a farm near where the Barlow Road forded the Sandy River. He built a bridge and a tollgate at the crossing. This became the second of the Barlow Road tollgates. It operated from 1853 to 1865.

After another long climb out of the valley, I rode into the town of Sandy. I had a quick lunch, refilled my water bottles, visited an ATM, and continued on. Highway 211 out of Sandy was one of the scariest roads I'd been on in a long time. No shoulders, lots of truck traffic, and drivers that weren't too inclined to give me three feet. I was glad this stretch was only five miles long.

At the intersection of Highway 211 and Highway 224 lies the historic Philip Foster farm. The farm remains in the hands of his descendants. Foster, if you recall, funded the initial construction of the Barlow Road. His farm was the emigrants' first contact with Willamette Valley civilization. Foster sold a substantial amount of fresh produce to the road-weary travelers as they emerged from the forest. Tours of his home are still regularly given but apparently just on Saturdays during the fall.

As the Barlow Road approached the Clackamas River it split into three branches. Each branch led to a different ford. The most popular crossing was near the west end of today's Southeast Folsom Road. The second favorite choice was near the current bridge at the community of Carver. Finally, the third ford was located near Barton Park, my campground for the night.

I turned north onto Highway 224. This road was a vast improvement over Highway 211. It was flat and had a nice shoulder. After three miles I arrived at Barton Park. The park is operated by Clackamas County and is perhaps the cleanest, best maintained public campground where I've ever stayed. The staff obviously puts a lot of pride into their work.

Tuesday, September 13th - Barton Park, OR, to Oregon City, OR - 12 miles

This was the day I'd been working towards for five years: the end of the Oregon Trail. It was a short, easy ride. Only twelve miles remained as I departed Barton Park. There were, however, a few more landmarks to see.

After crossing the Clackamas River, the three branches of the Barlow Road merged back together before entering Oregon City. I continued to follow the branch from Barton Park as it hugged the south bank of the Clackamas until I reached Carver. There I came to the historic Baker Cabin and Pioneer Church. Horace Baker and his wife, Jane, settled on this land in 1846. Horace had become so preoccupied with his business as a stone mason that, ten years later, he still hadn't found the time to build his wife a proper home. According to the Baker Cabin Historical Society, neighbors took pity on Jane and, in 1856, built this cabin for her. It sits on the original site and is unique because of its cantilevered loft. On the same property now rests the German Methodist Pioneer Church. It was built in 1895 and was originally located several miles away. In 1967 it was moved to its present location.

I made my way up one last long hill and then turned south onto Bradley Road. As I approached Holcomb Boulevard, I connected with the recombined Barlow Road. I turned west onto Holcomb and followed it all the way to the End of the Oregon Trail Interpretive Center in Oregon City. This truly was the end of the Oregon Trail. The museum was built on Abernethy Green. In the earliest years of emigration, overland travelers arrived in Oregon City at the onset of winter. They would often build temporary camps on Abernethy Green until spring when they could fan out and stake their land claims. When the Barlow Road opened in 1846, Abernethy Green was its official endpoint.

I was met at the museum by Dr. Jim Tompkins. He is a past President of the Northwest Chapter of OCTA, and also previously served on the Interpretive Center's Board of Directors. Dr. Tompkins and other museum staff gave me a personal, guided tour of the exhibits. It's an excellent museum and was a great way to end my journey.

As every cross-country bicycle tourist knows, the trip isn't officially over until you dip your wheel into the ocean. I had to improvise since I didn't actually do coast-to-coast. Way back in Independence, Missouri, five years before, I dipped my rear wheel into the Missouri River. All that remained now was to dip my front wheel into the Willamette River. In Oregon City there is a bike path that runs along the Willamette, past my hotel, to Clackamette Park. I positioned my bike so the front wheel was in the river then I snagged a pedestrian who was walking on the pathway. I handed him the camera, told him my story, and asked him to take the shot. I felt my journey was truly complete. I had bicycled the entire Oregon Trail.

My arrival at the End of the Oregon Trail Interpretive Center, Oregon City, Oregon. *45.364765, -122.594805*

There Are Lessons Here, Somewhere

One of my favorite old Charlie Brown holiday specials was the one where the Peanuts gang travels through France, touring the historic battlefields of WWI and WWII. Based in part on Charles Schulz's own experiences as a young soldier in the 1940s, it was the cartoonist at his very best. Near the end of the show, Linus asks a rhetorical question: "What Have We Learned, Charlie Brown?" So, to answer all the Linuses of the world, here's what I learned on the Oregon Trail.

The people that originally followed the trail were not heroes. Some performed heroic feats along the way, occasionally through altruism, but more often out of necessity. The line that separates heroism from survival is fuzzy at best. Although their specific reasons for heading west varied, the underlying goal was a better life. For some, that better life meant free land and a fresh start. For others, a better life meant freedom to worship without persecution. And, for many, gold was their goal. In these respects the emigrants of 170 years ago were not very different from people today.

What seems to separate our society from the pioneer society, however, is the extent to which the pioneers were willing to sacrifice to reach their goals. They did not wait for or expect someone to take care of their needs. Such expectations had no precedent. If they wanted a better life they knew it was up to them to achieve it. Somehow, somewhere, many among us have forgotten this simple fact. There was no free ride to Oregon then, and there is no free ride to a better life now.

The interactions between the emigrants and the Indians were, for the most part, peaceable. At first, tribes along the route viewed the wagon trains as traveling markets. Animal pelts, handmade baskets, and other readily available items could be traded with the pioneers for cloth, metal tools, and even firearms. The trade was beneficial to both sides. As more and more travelers passed through the Indians' traditional territories, the relations became increasingly strained. Resources were plundered, diseases were introduced, and confrontations became more violent. While attacks resembling what is portrayed in movies and on television were extremely rare, sporadic killings did occur on both sides. The number one cause of death along the trail, however, was illness. For three decades that fact never changed.

Firearms on the trail were very primitive. Pistols were rare, and almost all the long guns were muzzleloaders. This is why firearms accidents were so common. In order for the weapon to be available for immediate use, it had to be loaded in advance. It was a slow process. Powder had to be measured and poured down the barrel. Wadding, a lead ball, sometimes more wadding, and occasionally even wax then had to be rammed down the barrel. Finally, a percussion cap was put into place. All of these steps were necessary for a single shot. There were no safety mechanisms. If the hammer somehow struck the cap, *boom*! Another bump in the road.

It would be easy to conclude that the west was settled primarily by overland pioneers. In reality, less than half of the people who settled in California, Oregon, and Washington came by wagon. Until the completion of the Transcontinental Railroad, the majority of newcomers arrived by ship, first to San Francisco and then to smaller ports up and down the west coast. An ocean voyage to the Isthmus of Panama or around Cape Horn was no less dramatic than a wagon train but history, for some reason, overlooks the seafaring pioneers.

As I traveled the Oregon Trail, three questions were repeatedly asked by people I met along the way. First, "Aren't you afraid to be traveling alone?" Next, "Are you carrying a gun?" And finally, "How many flat tires have you had?"

I think some people, maybe most people, are afraid to be alone whether they are traveling or not. In the modern world we have become so accustomed to being connected to each other with cell phones, or social media, or whatever, that the idea of being alone seems unnatural. If you think about it though, being alone was not the norm for overland pioneers either. In fact, one of the biggest complaints recorded in emigrant journals was the lack of privacy. For me, however, traveling alone gave me time to really absorb my surroundings. I could take whatever time I wanted to smell the sage, listen to the coyotes, or contemplate the hardships of a half million people who walked the trail before me. Fear is a human reaction to the unknown. Proper planning goes a long way to eliminating the unknown and, thus, any fear that comes with it. I can honestly say I was not afraid to travel alone.

As for carrying a gun, the answer is "No." Although I fully support an individual's right to carry a gun, either openly or concealed, such a decision has to be made based on practical considerations. Bringing a pistol on this journey, I felt, wasn't worth the hassle. I didn't check baggage on any of my airline flights, so traveling to and from the trail with a gun would have been a logistical nightmare. Along the trail the concealed carry requirements vary from state to state. Oregon, for example, doesn't even have reciprocity with Louisiana. No, a gun on this trip would have just made things more complicated than they needed to be.

Flat tires are a perennial problem for many bicycle tourists. I know one guy who rode along the Columbia River on the Interstate and had eight flats in one day. Luck plays some part in avoiding punctures but choosing a quality tire is equally important. High pressure, lightweight, skinny road tires go flat if you look at them wrong. My tires had significantly more rubber on them than most bicycle tires. They were 2" wide and I kept the pressure at 45-50 psi. Also, I was very lucky. Over the course of 2,475 miles I only had one flat tire. That has to be some sort of record.

There are lessons to be learned in every adventure we allow ourselves to undertake. Mark Twain once said, "Twenty years from now you will be more disappointed by the things that you didn't do than by the ones you did do. So throw off the bowlines. Sail away from the safe harbor. Catch the trade winds in your sails. Explore. Dream. Discover." At 56, I'm still proud to admit "I don't know what I want to do when I grow up." I even worked that phrase into my retirement ceremony from the Air Force Reserves. I'm not advocating aimless wandering but "growing up" implies you've stopped growing. In nature, when an organism stops growing, stagnation sets in. Stagnation is the first stage of death. Yes, we all die, but there is no reason not to keep growing until the very end. The pioneers saw the Oregon Trail as their pathway to a better life. Metaphorically speaking, it can still be seen that way. Lessons remain to be discovered by modern explorers of the trail. Discovery and growth go hand-in-hand and both continue to be pathways to a better life.

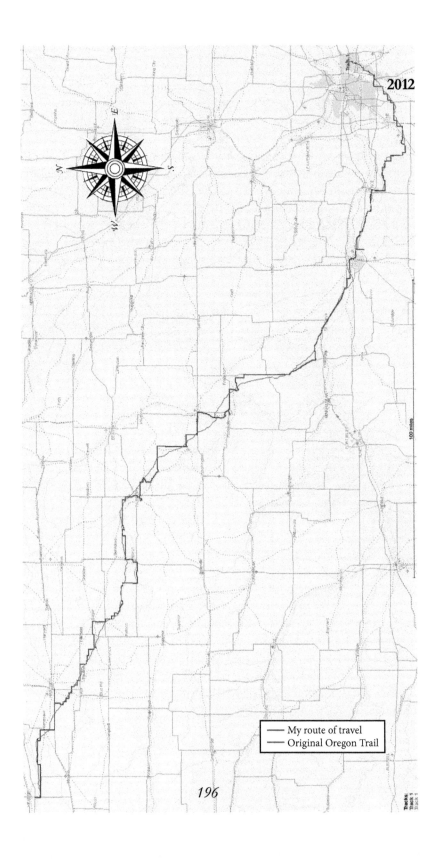

2012

My route of travel
Original Oregon Trail

GPS Coordinates of Selected Oregon Trail Landmarks

Note that the following landmarks are not arranged in alphabetical order, but sequentially as if traveling the Oregon Trail from east to west. The GPS coordinates are all expressed in digital degrees. If you're not familiar with digital coordinates, simply type the numbers EXACTLY as written below into a program such as Google Earth, Google Maps, or Bing Maps. Hit "search" and the program will take you to that location.

Missouri

Wayne City Overlook	39.135167, -94.424758
Independence Court House Square	39.092481, -94.416462
Jim Bridger Grave	39.097955, -94.470771
National Frontier Trails Museum	39.086723, -94.419559
Santa Fe Park	39.065443, -94.426358
Manchester Ruts	38.970417, -94.498389
Blue River Crossing	38.926101, -94.571813
New Santa Fe Village	38.906671, -94.605856

Kansas

Lone Elm Park	38.822493, -94.830334
Gardner Junction	38.796433, -94.961717
Blue Mound	38.904468, -95.182607
Wakarusa Crossing	38.914911, -95.233510
Oregon Trail Park	39.229283, -96.152473
Vieux Crossing	39.256431, -96.249813
Scott Springs	39.383245, -96.405689
Black Vermillion River (lower crossing)	39.646756, -96.496109
Alcove Spring	39.749821, -96.678963

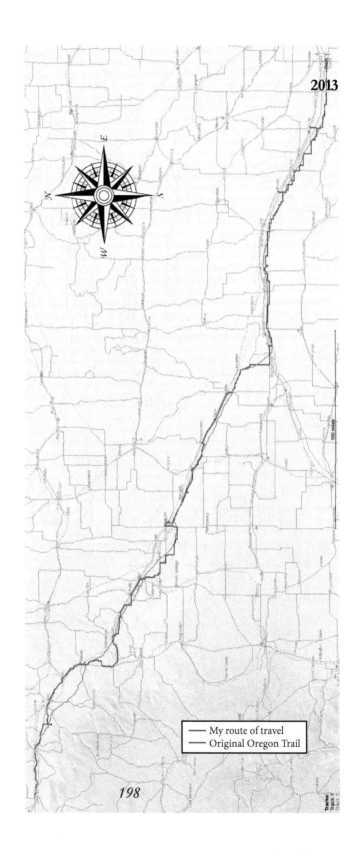

2013

My route of travel
Original Oregon Trail

198

| Hollenberg Pony Express Station | 39.900933, -96.843821 |

Nebraska

Rock Creek Pony Express Station	40.113167, -97.060190
George Winslow Grave	40.207618, -97.206188
Kiowa Station	40.227021, -97.756896
Oak Grove Station	40.230662, -97.873505
The Narrows, Little Blue River	40.252725, -97.929811
Pawnee Ranch	40.398557, -98.226039
Indian Hollow	40.480143, -98.392182
Susan Haile Grave	40.655325, -98.713367
Fort Kearny State Historic Site	40.642730, -99.006082
Plum Creek Massacre Site	40.671113, -99.576940
Plum Creek Cemetery	40.672693, -99.605975
Fort McPherson Soldier Statue	41.016483, -100.517837
Fort McPherson National Cemetery	41.024809, -100.524673
Sioux Lookout	41.059088, -100.645854
O'Fallons Bluff	41.137668, -101.096606
California Crossing	41.079226, -101.955152
California Hill	41.098799, -101.978416
Windlass Hill	41.261777, -102.115733
Ash Hollow	41.295442, -102.123241
Rachel Pattison Grave	41.308029, -102.125478
Signal Bluff	41.335825, -102.227713
John Hollman Grave	41.377887, -102.347827
Frog Rock	41.518663, -102.655632
Amanda Lamme marker	41.612861, -103.003701
Courthouse and Jail Rocks	41.596793, -103.114119
Chimney Rock	41.703889, -103.348064
Rebecca Winters Grave	41.843199, -103.617119
Scott's Bluff	41.836940, -103.700307
Mitchell Pass	41.830105, -103.712778
Robidoux Pass	41.814757, -103.850442

Wyoming

Grattan Battlefield marker	42.132305, -104.405671
Platte River Bridge	42.210398, -104.533378
Fort Laramie National Historic Site	42.202696, -104.557496
Mary Homsley Grave	42.221534, -104.566407
Register Cliff	42.248444, -104.710447

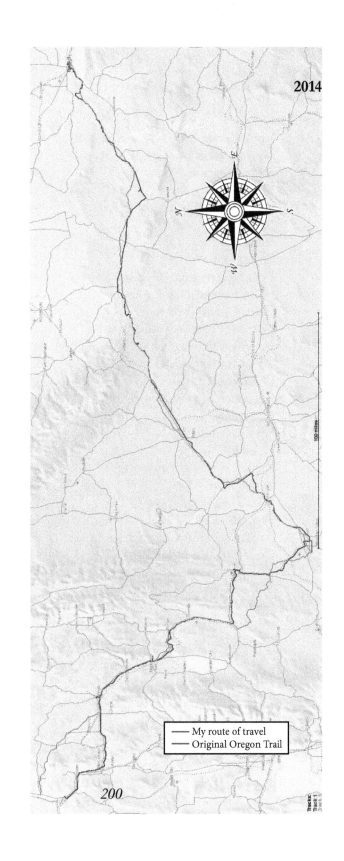

2014

My route of travel
Original Oregon Trail

100 miles

200

Guernsey Ruts	42.255938, -104.748402
Warm Springs	42.249347, -104.780866
Laramie Peak	42.267091, -105.442968
Joel Hembree Grave	42.752171, -105.600461
Ayres Natural Bridge	42.734260, -105.612152
Alvah Unthank Grave	42.825869, -105.790260
The Rock in the Glen	42.860084, -105.884389
Reshaw Bridge Site	42.870220, -106.267234
BLM National Historic Trails Interpretive Center	
	42.866277, -106.337146
Emigrant Gap	42.844563, -106.539007
Red Buttes Crossing	42.771912, -106.530799
The Devil's Backbone	42.736833, -106.661897
Clayton's Slough	42.712916, -106.695746
Willow Springs	42.674857, -106.793662
Prospect Hill	42.660403, -106.810202
Horse Creek Station	42.604274, -106.965267
Independence Rock	42.493619, -107.131779
Devil's Gate	42.448696, -107.209971
Frederick Fulkerson Grave	42.443879, -107.206729
Martin's Cove / Sun Ranch Historic Site	
	42.442509, -107.218520
Martin's Cove	42.453862, -107.239240
Split Rock	42.480671, -107.529533
Split Rock BLM Site	42.453300, -107.545864
Split Rock marker	42.472888, -107.604106
Ice Slough	42.518280, -108.009896
Sixth Crossing	42.510018, -108.231454
Seventh and Eighth Crossings (approximate)	
	42.494312, -108.286178
Rocky Ridge, Lower Monument	42.470931, -108.409611
Rocky Ridge, Upper Monument	42.462892, -108.437026
Radium Springs	42.447779, -108.509739
Gillespie Place	42.449846, -108.509144
Rock Creek Hollow	42.436712, -108.621929
Burnt Ranch / Ninth Crossing	42.376697, -108.716885
Twin Mounds	42.348097, -108.837401
South Pass	42.343129, -108.886972
Pacific Springs	42.336907, -108.939606
Charlotte Dansie Grave	42.301292, -108.987602

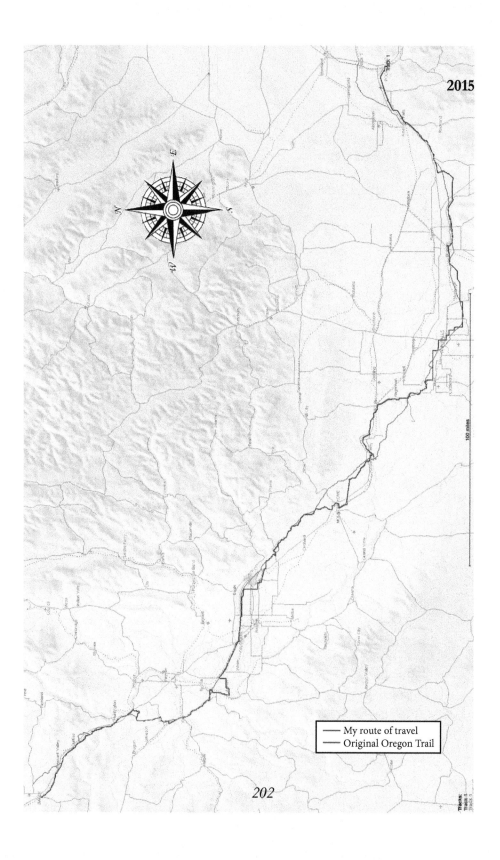

My route of travel
Original Oregon Trail

False Parting of the Ways	42.284889, -109.059107
True Parting of the Ways	42.257893, -109.228066
Big Sandy Crossing	42.109496, -109.449688
Simpson's Hollow	42.017918, -109.590821
Lombard Crossing	41.880066, -109.807602
Daniel Lantz Grave	41.628624, -109.905366
Granger Station	41.590546, -109.969907
Church Butte	41.505243, -110.135363
Fort Bridger	41.318621, -110.393408
Cumberland Gap	41.583154, -110.567870

Idaho

Thomas Fork	42.213677, -111.069773
Big Hill	42.230156, -111.196996
Hooper Springs	42.678991, -111.603741
Wagon Box Grave	42.656592, -111.606972
Sheep Rock	42.644399, -111.707002
Hudspeth Cutoff marker	42.629874, -111.917357
Fish Creek Summit	42.625751, -111.920675
Fort Hall Replica	42.844051, -112.420192
Fort Hall Original Site	43.020184, -112.634556
American Falls	42.776557, -112.875170
Hell's Gate / Massacre Rocks	42.674598, -112.987231
Register Rock	42.652702, -113.016914
Cold Water Hill	42.615541, -113.140350
Raft River marker	42.577106, -113.219340
Raft River Parting of the Ways	42.571485, -113.236883
Stricker Store and Station	42.460374, -114.323184
Kanaka Rapids	42.665184, -114.802000
Thousand Springs	42.747028, -114.842907
Three Island Crossing	42.935611, -115.333152
Canyon Creek Station	43.262061, -115.703598
Inscription Rock (#1)	43.362553, -115.803871
Ditto Creek Station (approximate site)	43.375349, -115.817792
Inscription Rock (#2)	43.397542, -115.849605
Mayfield Station	43.418193, -115.898338
Bonneville Point	43.491806, -116.040389
Ward Massacre Memorial Park	43.677186, -116.608797
Boise River Crossing	43.688992, -116.686240
Old Fort Boise (replica)	43.780040, -116.932472

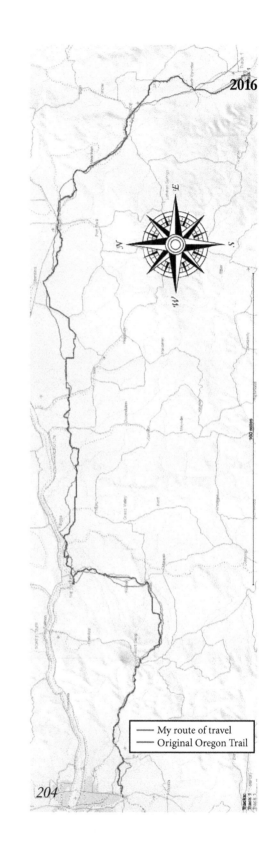

2016

My route of travel
Original Oregon Trail

Old Fort Boise (approximate site)	43.813089, -117.020055

Oregon

Starvation Camp marker	43.800054, -117.055424
Keeney Pass	43.911143, -117.177800
John D. Henderson Grave	43.972546, -117.235914
Alkali Springs	44.111168, -117.235262
Tub Springs	44.136835, -117.246949
Willow Creek Pioneer Camp	44.234855, -117.259046
Farewell Bend	44.306628, -117.224262
Van Ornum Massacre Site	44.333759, -117.245857
BLM Oregon Trail Interpretive Center	
	44.813902, -117.728533
Lone Tree (approximate site)	44.852502, -117.787218
Ladd Hill	45.216091, -117.987701
Hilgard Junction	45.342023, -118.233816
Blue Mountains Summit (I-84)	45.463083, -118.386200
Emigrant Springs	45.540883, -118.464213
Deadman Pass	45.599751, -118.506832
Corral Springs marker	45.697928, -119.132040
David Koontz Grave	45.736576, -119.187987
Fort Henrietta Park	45.741716, -119.198301
Echo Meadows	45.719759, -119.309541
Well Springs	45.632306, -119.706822
Well Springs Pioneer Cemetery	45.632720, -119.715771
Cecil Store	45.618358, -119.959728
Four Mile Canyon	45.622039, -120.044090
Weatherford Oregon Trail marker	45.622410, -120.165360
McDonald Ford	45.589439, -120.409045
Biggs Arch	45.657800, -120.862816
Chenoweth Creek / The Dalles	45.634266, -121.200556
Barlow Road Tollgate #1	45.181027, -121.380482
Fort Deposit (possible site, Barlow Cr. / White R.)	
	45.215180, -121.607838
Fort Deposit (possible site, Klinger's Camp)	
	45.244618, -121.630154
Fort Deposit (possible site, Devil's Half Acre)	
	45.273316, -121.679335
Barlow Pass	45.282915, -121.684683
Pioneer Woman's Grave	45.281922, -121.700320

Summit Meadows	45.283953, -121.736696
Pioneer Cemetery	45.284692, -121.737691
Barlow Road Tollgate #3	45.286311, -121.737631
Laurel Hill Chute #1 (approximate)	45.307580, -121.794804
Laurel Hill Chute #2 (approximate)	45.308689, -121.798031
Laurel Hill Chute #3	45.310793, -121.800390
Laurel Hill Chutes #4 and #5	45.306536, -121.823591
Barlow Road Tollgate #4	45.309356, -121.837471
Barlow Road Tollgate #5	45.319759, -121.903435
Barlow Road Tollgate #2	45.409520, -122.237945
Philip Foster Farm	45.358461, -122.354992
Clackamas River upper crossing	45.327802, -122.381430
Clackamas River middle crossing	45.380834, -122.412307
Clackamas River lower crossing	45.392724, -122.497301
Baker Cabin and Pioneer Church	45.390105, -122.496604
End of the Oregon Trail Interpretive Center	
	45.364765, -122.594805

And Speaking of Equipment

As a bicyclist myself, I know how other cyclists drool over equipment lists. So here is a partial list of the gear I used or carried with me along the Oregon Trail. I'm not necessarily endorsing any of these items or brands over another. I'm simply acknowledging what worked for me.

Bicycle

Frame and Fork	- Haro ICS 3.0 aluminum hardtail mountain bike frame with a rigid steel Salsa fork (2012)
	- Thorn Sherpa MK3 steel touring frame and fork (2013 - 2016)
Wheels	- Sun Rhyno Lite 26" rims with 32 spoke Shimano Deore hubs
Brakes	- Shimano Deore V-brakes
Tires	- Schwalbe Marathon Dureme 26x2.0
Crankset	- Shimano Alivio 22-32-42 square taper
Chain	- Shimano HG-93, 9-speed
Cassette	- Shimano HG-50 9-speed 11-34
Derailleurs	- Shimano Deore front and rear
Shifters	- Shimano Deore Rapid Fire 9-speed (rear)
	- Rivendell Silver downtube friction shifter (front)
Pedals	- MKS Lambda platform pedals
Fenders	- SKS Chromoplastic P-55
Tail lights	- Planet Bike SuperFlash Turbo (2)
Headlight	- Light & Motion Urban 550

Trailer, Racks, and Panniers

Trailer	- ExtraWheel Voyager with added top rack
Rear Rack	- Bruce Gordon rear rack
Front Rack	- Tubus Duo
Panniers	- ExtraWheel Expert Panniers, 80 liter capacity (pair)
Rear Rack Bag	- Arkel Tailrider

Camping Gear

Tent	- Kelty Gunnison 2.1
Sleeping Bag	- Kelty Light Year down filled 30°F
Bag liner	- Jag Bag Silk
Pad	- Therm-a-Rest ProLite
Stove	- Jetboil Flash

Clothing

Shorts (2)	- Louis Garneau baggy mountain bike shorts
T-shirts	- Under Armour loose fit heat gear (3)
LS shirt	- Cabellas long sleeve fishing shirt
Trousers	- Magellan lightweight convertible trousers
Base Layer	- Minus 39 merino wool top and bottom
Rain Jacket	- Showers Pass Storm Jacket
Rain Pants	- Showers Pass Storm Pants
Helmet Cover	- Jannd Stormtech
Shoes	- New Balance 928 walking shoes
Sandals	- Teva Hurricane

Hygiene

Toothbrush	- Whatever was available
Toothpaste	- Ditto
Soap	- One bar of Ivory soap, used for body and hair and an occasional dish or utensil
Towel	- Large microfiber towel (corner used as washcloth when shaving)
Razor	- Bar soap used instead of shaving cream

| Baby Wipes | - Used whenever showers weren't available; also used as toilet paper (no reason to carry both) |

Food

Breakfast	- Instant Grits, Instant Oatmeal, Breakfast Bars
Lunch	- Usually at a diner or café if possible
Supper	- Peanut Butter, tortillas

Miscellaneous

Food bag	- Grub Pack model "A" small (rodent proof)
Solar Charger	- Suntactics sCharger-5
GPS	- Garmin eTrex Vista H (b&w screen)
Camera	- Canon Powershot S120
Compass	- Silva Polaris
Map App	- Back Country Navigator Pro for Android
Tablets	- Samsung Galaxy 7 (2012 - 2014)
	- Verizon Ellipsis (2015 until I lost it)
	- LG 7 (2015 replacement)

Bibliography

Bagley, Will. *So Rugged and Mountainous: Blazing the Trails to Oregon and California 1812-1848.* Norman: University of Oklahoma Press, 2010.

— *South Pass.* Norman: University of Oklahoma Press, 2014.

— *With Golden Visions Bright Before Them: Trails to the Mining West 1849-1852.* Norman: University of Oklahoma Press, 2012.

Becher, Ronald. *Massacre Along the Medicine Road: A Social History of the Indian War of 1864 in Nebraska Territory.* Caldwell, Idaho: Caxton Press, 1999.

Coffman, Lloyd W. *Blazing a Wagon Trail to Oregon: A Weekly Chronicle of the Great Migration of 1843.* Caldwell, Idaho: Caxton Press, 2012.

Dawson, Charles. *Pioneer Tales of the Oregon Trail and of Jefferson County.* Topeka, Kansas: Crane and Company, 1912.

Franzwa, Gregory M. *The Oregon Trail Revisited.* Tucson, Arizona: The Patrice Press, 1997.

McLynn, Frank. *Wagons West: The Epic Story of America's Overland Trails.* New York: Grove Press, 2002.

Meeker, Ezra and Howard R. Driggs. *Ox Team Days on the Oregon Trail*. Yonkers-on-Hudson, New York and Chicago, Illinois: World Book Company, 1922.

Parkman, Francis Jr. *The Oregon Trail*. 1847. Reprint, Umpqua, Oregon: River Canyon Press, 2010.

Rea, Tom. *Devil's Gate: Owning the Land, Owning the Story*. Norman: University of Oklahoma Press, 2006.

Roberts, David. *Devil's Gate: Brigham Young and the Great Mormon Handcart Tragedy*. New York: Simon and Shuster, 2008.

Shannon, Donald H. *The Boise Massacre on the Oregon Trail*. Caldwell, Idaho: Snake Country Publishing, 2004.

Stark, Peter. *Astoria: John Jacob Astor and Thomas Jefferson's Lost Pacific Empire*. New York: Ecco, 2014.

Tompkins, Jim. *Discovering Laurel Hill and the Barlow Road*. Accessed August 15, 2016. http://www.octa-trails.org/media/dynamic/files/168_Barlow_Road_Guidebook.pdf.

Unruh, John D. Jr. *The Plains Across: The Overland Emigrants and the Trans-Mississippi West, 1840-60*. 1979. Reprint, Urbana and Chicago: University of Illinois Press, 1993.

Wasco County and Clackamas County Historical Societies. *Barlow Road, Bicentennial Edition 1974-1975*. 4th ed. Portland, Oregon: J. Y. Hollingsworth Company, 1985.

CPSIA information can be obtained
at www.ICGtesting.com
Printed in the USA
LVOW05s1747260517
535607LV00005B/7/P